Marvelous Reality:

The Fascination of
South America

Marvelous Reality:
The Fascination of South America

James W. Reid

Holland America
A TRADITION OF EXCELLENCE

ACKNOWLEDGEMENTS

I wish to express my profound gratitude to the many people who have so graciously cooperated in providing materials for this book, and to the private collectors who have provided illustrations from their collections of Pre-Columbian, South American colonial and modern art. I am especially indebted to His Royal Highness Prince Philip, the Duke of Edinburgh, for permission to reproduce the South Atlantic landscape painting by Edward Seago.

Dr Jorge Glusberg, Director of the Museo Nacional de Bellas Artes in Buenos Aires, graciously authorized the reproduction of two superb paintings by Rembrandt van Rijn and Amadeo Modigliani in the Museum's collection. PRO CHILE, the Chilean Trade Commission in New York, was most helpful in furnishing color slides originating from SERNATUR, the Chilean Servicio Nacional de Turismo. In Uruguay, my thanks go to Joaquín Ragni, Presidente, Asociación Amigos del Museo Juan Manuel Blanes, who coordinated details regarding Uruguayan art. Gabriel Beluffo, Director of the Museo Municipal de Bellas Artes Juan Manuel Blanes, kindly permitted reproduction of two important paintings by Juan Manuel Blanes from the Museum's collection.

Many old friends have made invaluable contributions. Don Alberto Bildner, who knows Brazil as well as anybody, provided invaluable insights regarding *Carioca* life. Millicent Maas Dunham drew my attention to the less well-known work by Rudyard Kipling, including his sea shanty about Rió de Janeiro. Alfredo Fellinger gave me the benefit of his eclectic knowledge about Argentina, and especially about the writer Echeverría. Malcolm Alexander (Alexander Global Promotions, WA) was instrumental in seeing that the project was done in a highly professional manner, and Dave Patterson gave scrupulous attention to producing superb maps.

I wish also to express my appreciation to A.K. Lanterman for his thoughtful Preface, and to Bill Pedlar, Anne Wagner and Pat Ferraro for helping to bring the project to fruition. I am grateful to Pascal Reid for bringing all his technical skills in multi-media methodologies to bear in unraveling e-mail dispatches of texts overseas. Lastly, special thanks goes to Riet Vandenboorn for unfailing patience and technical skill in all phases of computer work associated with this book.

A final debt of gratitude is due to the many writers and poets whose works in the realm of *belles-lettres*, historic research, travel narratives and critical analysis have enriched understanding of the South American continent and have served as an inspiration in the preparation of this book.

Illustration Credits
PRO CHILE, New York and SERNATUR (Chilean Servicio Nacional de Turismo): page 15 (bottom), page 90, page 94 (middle). Museo Nacional de Bellas Artes, Buenos Aires, Argentina: page 141 (top and bottom). Museo Municipal de Bellas Artes Juan Manuel Blanes, Prado, Montevideo, Uruguay: page 160 (bottom), page 161. Jian Chen: page 16 (top), page 77, page 79, page 91 (top), page 154 (bottom), page 162. Lyle Wachovsky: page 154 (top). James W. Reid: other illustrations and line drawings.

*   *   *

Produced by Alexander Global Promotions
Edited by May Holdsworth
Printed in China
ISBN 0-9675934-0-9

For
Toby and Garcilaso
faithful companions and loyal friends
in adventures in the High Andes
and in travels through life

PREFACE

The 127 years during which Holland America ships have carried international passengers have provided unparalleled opportunities to make travel experiences both more enjoyable and more meaningful. Our belief is that, as the French philosopher Montesquieu once observed, bringing one's mind into contact with those of people of other nations and continents is invaluable in enhancing civilized relations.

Understanding a nation's *gestalt*—what makes it what it is, and what distinguishes it—is a vital part of this process. We believe that travel overseas is immensely enriched when the traveler returns with new insights, new perspectives and new horizons. What this implies is the simultaneous assimilation and appreciation of an ensemble of kaleidoscopic experiences: topography, flora and fauna; political, military, economic, social, religious and historical backgrounds; and the music, literature, art and archaeology by which peoples express their intellectual and aesthetic beliefs.

James W. Reid, the founder of our Flagship Forum cultural enrichment program, has epitomized this thinking in the more than 1,000 presentations which he has delivered for Holland America. Over the years, we have discovered that the passengers who attend his lectures, and those of other distinguished speakers, wish not only to have an orientation guide for their cruise, but also to gain special insights into the places visited. *Marvelous Reality: The Fascination of South America* is intended to do precisely that. It focuses upon the countries and places visited in our South American Cruises, and will, we hope, be a memorable memento of your adventures in this extraordinary continent.

Few people have the unusual intellectual, academic and practical knowledge of South America possessed by James Reid. Fewer still have the ability to communicate the continent's excitement in such an absorbing, sophisticated and enthusiastic manner. We hope that you will find his book, with its rich images and discerning insights, a very special source of enjoyment.

A.K. Lanterman
Chairman and CEO

CONTENTS

U.S.A.

ATLANTIC OCEAN

GULF OF MEXICO

Ft. Lauderdale

Grand Cayman

CARIBBEAN SEA

CENTRAL AMERICA

San Blas Islands

Panama Canal

Balboa

Manta/Quito

EQUATOR

The Amazon

GALAPAGOS ISLANDS

Callao/Lima/Machu Picchu

SOUTH AMERICA

General San Martín/ Pisco/Nazca Lines

Arica

Iguazu Falls

EASTER ISLAND

Rio de Janeiro

A sultry city where the operative word is...samba!

Bet on a good time at the elegant casino in Viña del Mar.

The place to try *yerba maté*, traditional tea of the gauchos.

Coquimbo

Valparaíso

Santiago

Buenos Aires

Montevideo

PACIFIC

N
W E
S

OCEAN

Puerto Montt

Stroll Avenida 9 de Julio, the widest street in the world.

0   1,000   2,000
KILOMETERS

Charted by Magellan in 1520 on the first ever around-the-world cruise.

FALKLAND ISLANDS

Chilean Passage

Watch for sea lions, dolphins and orca whales.

Strait of Magellan

Stanley

Are they British, or Argentine? It depends upon whom you ask.

Punta Arenas

Ushuaia, Tierra del Fuego

Beagle Channel

Cape Horn

The southernmost city in the world.

Charted by Charles Darwin on his exploratory cruise in 1832.

ANTARCTICA

An unusual "shore excursion" as you flightsee over the White Continent from Punta Arenas.

Latin America's Marvelous Reality

The Marvel of the Real

Travel to faraway places will be "full of adventure, full of discovery," the 20th-century Greek poet of Alexandria, Constantin Cavafy tells us,

> As long as you keep your thoughts raised high,
> as long as a rare excitement
> stirs your spirit and your body.

Rare excitement! This is something that few places can conjure up as dramatically as does South America, a continent which for the great 20th-century Cuban writer Alejo Carpentier embodied "the marvel of the real." For here was "a world of kings crowned with green plumes, of primeval vegetation, of brews drawn from cacti and palm trees,". . . "of the Promethean solitude of Bolívar in Santa Marta, the battles waged for nine hours at sword point in the lunar landscapes of the Andes, the towers of Tikal. . ." Here indeed the lines of demarcation blur between truth and fantasy. Between the normal and the miraculous, and between the natural and the supernatural.

The Greek poet Constantin Cavafy, in one of his celebrated poems, wrote: "Hope the voyage is a long one . . . May there be many a summer morning when, with what pleasure, what joy, you come into harbors seen for the first time."

Majestic Topography

It is the majestic topography which most overtly incarnates this marvelous reality. There is a transcendental splendor to the exhilarating vistas of the Pacific desert coast, the ethereal beauty of snow-capped peaks and mighty glaciers, the awe-inspiring volcanoes soaring above tranquil lakes, the solitary remoteness of the Chilean fjords, the magical perfection of a double rainbow arching over windswept Cape Horn, the Wagnerian grandeur of thundering Iguazú Falls, and the lavish exuberance of tropical Amazonia. Vast distances and huge uninhabited expanses inspire the traveler to contemplation and meditation, while the intriguing towns and cities in between summon up the pervasive legacies of the past and the omnipresent pageant of the present.

Flora and Fauna

A giant of Latin American literature, the Cuban Alejo Carpentier first used the term lo real maravilloso or "the marvel of the real" about South America.

Diverse flora and fauna dwell in these terrains. There are strangely shaped fruits like *chirimoyas*, exotic vermilion orchids in viridian jungle vegetation, noble trees like the Argentine *ombu* and the *ceiba* of

French poet Leconte de Lisle, whose famous poem Le Sommeil du Condor (The Sleep of the Condor) refers to 19th-century European fascination with a mysterious, inaccessible world where the condor, higher up in the Andes than the regions of "Mists haunted by black eagles . . . contemplates America and its immensity in silence," and "sleeps in the icy air, with his vast wings."

Tikal, and the marine kelp that gave its name to the people of the Falkland Islands. Compelling creatures abound: coatis in Argentina and Brazil, toucans of lavishly opulent and varied plumage, the fastidious camelids of the High Andes, gargantuan sea elephants of southern South America, and ingratiating penguins.

The mighty condor, with wing spans of 15 feet, would inspire a French 19th-century poet, Leconte de Lisle, to pen a memorable poem: *Le Sommeil du Condor* (*The Sleep of the Condor*).

This has always been a fantastic world. Where else in the American past would one encounter such strange manifestations of culture as the extraordinary erotic art of the Moches, the presentation ceremony to the Lord of Sipán with blood-filled goblets, the colossal stone edifices shaped with primitive tools, a graphic art whose simultaneous use of figurative and abstract motifs was rare in the Western world until 1900? Imagine ongoing annual parades of Inca mummy bundles, an empire of 15 million people conquered by the ruthless Francisco Pizarro with a mere 100 men, and hardened conquistadors so apprehensive that the cloth spun and woven by Andean women symbolized a potentially inimical sorcery that textiles embellished with feathers were officially banned in 1550. And for centuries men mesmerized by visions of El Dorado persisted in hopeless quests to find its fabled wealth.

Spinning is an enduring tradition. The early 19th-century Spanish chronicler Garcilaso de la Vega said Andean women "were so accumstomed to spinning that they brought their spindles out onto the streets . . . when they were on the way to see a friend, and they kept on working after they reached her house, while they were chatting together."

Amazing personages emerge: the giant Indians discovered by Magellan, whose invocations to Setebos would inspire Shakespeare; the archangels with arquebuses who became a salient motif of Spanish colonial religious art, an art to which Indian painters also added imaginary plazas of Spanish cities and sinister inquisitors presiding over *auto da fé* burnings at the stake in the name of the Catholic faith. How can we

Between 1550 and 1820, the centuries of Spanish Viceroyalty rule of South America apart from Brazil, indigenous artists contributed their own iconographic images, like the archangel with arquebus.

not be awed by San Martín's incredible crossing of the lofty snow-capped Andes from Argentina to Chile with poorly equipped troops, who nevertheless defeated the regular Spanish forces? The 19th century contributed its own fantastic personalities: the dictator Melgarego giving his horse buckets of beer; monarchs who ruled from Rió and summered in Petropolis, the religious fanatic O Conselheiro and his followers engaging the Brazilian army in pitched battles, and, in Chile's remote southern Punta Arenas, immigrant tycoons from Europe paying bounties for Indian ears and testicles.

In our time, the marvel of the real has been especially apparent in forms of visual expression. A remarkable triangular bronze-tinted Cathedral in Rió resembles a Maya temple, and at Brasilia a phenomenal space age city became the new national capital in 1960. In Chile the Legislature, an avant-garde geometric structure, is in Valparaiso, even though the Executive and Judiciary remain an hour away, in Santiago. Two Latin American artists, Rufino Tamayo and Wifredo Lam, delivered an authentic surrealism that, unlike the artificially contrived compositions of such European artists as Magritte, executed works of hallucinatory beauty and compelling color, whose authenticity stemmed from ancient beliefs and rituals, and from the exotic jungle milieu. And such South American deities of the past as *Pachamama*, the Earth Mother, too, are implicit in Fernando Botero's marvelously ample sculptures of well rounded forms.

As for literature, where else in the world in the 20th century has there been such an explosion of talent as that of South America's boom of the 1950s and 1960s? Who can equal the "magical realist" inventions of Gabriel García Marquez, in *One Hundred Years of Solitude*, *Love in the Time of Cholera* or *The Autumn of the Patiarch*, such as Remedios the Beauty suddenly ascending into the sky, a solitary cow ruminating on the balcony of the Presidential Palace, a liner floating across a city?

Author's sketch of a detail of a sculpture by Fernando Botero, the Colombian artist born in 1932. The monumental scale and fullness of form of the work itself evoke the tradition of South America's ancient Pachamama or Earth Mother.

Rituals

Rituals, festivals, parades, *Carnaval* . . . here is a bygone world, constantly reenacted in a contemporary setting. From the western coast of South America, across the Andes to Brazil and thence to Cuba's Santeria, the shaman, *curandero*, witch doctor and Exu hold sway. In the Brazilian *Terreiro* temples of Candomblé, mediums communicate with gods of the past; during the Jemanjá festival, possessed figures float in the sea and, at the time of the annual Bomfím procession, white-laced mulattas solemnly wash the steps to the church. Often, pagan beliefs blend with Catholic liturgies, as in Bolivia's La Diablada Festival in Oruro, when dancing figures don the attire of condors and thereby assume the power of the great-spanned monarch of the Andes. Horsemen still rule the great flat plains known as the pampa: in Chile *huasos*, and in Argentina gauchos, of casual attire and resplendent silver money belts. And in tropical Amazonia some 150 different Stone Age peoples like the Kaiapos and Yanomanis continue to celebrate rites of passage as they have for the past thousand years.

The 20th century has produced its own realities, some marvelous and some macabre, but always amazing. A Mexican civil war from 1910 to 1920 could see two out of 16 million people die, yet still produce the first truly populist agrarian leader, the charismatic Emiliano Zapata. In the 1930s, the improbable Lampião, of scholarly aspect, terrorized northeastern Brazil with hundreds of mounted bandits, until he was killed, and his head preserved in a museum jar. In 1979, two highly civilized "European" South American countries, Argentina and Chile, were ready to fight a war over three forlorn rocky outcrops at the entrance to the Beagle Channel and were only persuaded to desist by the timely intervention of the papal emissary. No one, however, could stop the war that never should have happened, the 1982 Falkland Islands conflict launched by an Argentine military triumvirate that was dazzled by imaginary glories in the past. These glories faded rapidly when reality intervened—the reality of a 70-ship armada dispatched from ports more than 8,000 miles away by a lady, British Prime Minister Margaret Thatcher.

Differences from the U.S.

South and North America have always been different. This can be attributed to the southern continent's predilection for fantasy, the focus on tradition and belief in miracles, and North America's pragmatism and determination to forge a new world. In South America, there were sophisticated old cultures based on agricultural or urban structures; in the north the Indians were essentially nomads. In the south, Indians accustomed to unilateral chains of command acquired a Spanish sovereign as ruler, in lieu of the Inca; in the north, immigrants came, not to perpetuate the decadent monarchies of Europe, but to forge new systems of government. This meant that the stimuli for colonization and development were very different. While South America remained largely cut off from the Age of Reason, North America embraced the ideas of the Enlightenment, emphasizing the rights of man and the political pluralism that eluded their South American counterparts.

The independence movements in North and South America engendered notable differences. South American liberators like Simón Bolívar and José de San Martín were professional military men, and that tradition came to be perpetuated in the form of government by *caudillo*— strongman rule, much of it dictatorial, spiced with instability and characterized

Simón Bolívar (1783-1830), Venezuelan soldier-statesman who achieved independence for six Latin American republics by freeing them from the Spanish yoke.

by *de facto* removal of one ruler by another by *golpes*, or *coups d'état*. In North America, by contrast, "citizen soldiers" and *de jure* constitutionally elected governments were the norm. In place of South America's often dogmatic religious intolerance, combined with strong religious influences in government, North America encouraged freedom of religion and a clear separation of church and state.

South America until the mid-19th-century advent of Juan Domingo Perón remained rurally oriented, with a corollary emphasis on primary products, while the United States was urban and oriented to industry and technology. What all of this meant is that in such matters as education, the status of women and human rights, South America tended to lag far behind North America. But South America, the Uruguayan writer Rodó argued in *Ariel* in the early 1900s, could take solace from the fact that it was more cultured and civilized, and less pragmatically materialist than its North American neighbor.

MERCOSUL/MERCOSUR: Dynamic New Economic Union

The differences have narrowed since then. Across the Andes, from sultry Rió de Janeiro to Santiago de Chile, new winds are blowing, epitomized by MERCOSUL, the Brazilian/Portuguese spelling for the economic union that Spanish-speaking South Americans call MERCOSUR. Created in 1991 by the Treaty of Asunción, it links Brazil, Argentina, Paraguay, Uruguay, Bolivia and Chile as a free trade area designed to establish a common market and serve as a platform for integration into the world economy. Embracing well over 200 million people, and with a Gross Domestic Product of over $1 trillion, it is in effect the South American equivalent of NAFTA and the European Union. Just as important is that this economic union is a catalyst of recent trends favoring political pluralism, since only countries with democratically elected governments are eligible for membership.

Approaching South America: The Excitement of Anticipation

South America thus provides a broad spectrum of interests and activities, likely to beguile people searching for new horizons in history, culture, nature and of course unusual shopping opportunities! The ideal way to travel there is by ship, to permit oneself to adapt gradually to a profoundly different continent and way of life. Such voyages are equally exciting, whether the route is through the Caribbean past Devil's Island, through the Panama Canal, or down the west coast, stopping to savor the wonders of ancient Tikal. Whatever one's route, the anticipation of South America's marvelous reality will surely engender that "rare excitement" which Constantine Cavafy encouraged all travelers to experience.

The majestic panorama of Iguazú Falls seen from the Brazilian side.

Navigating amid the splendor of Laguna San Rafael, in southern Chile.

A rare example of South American
erotic art: a Moche ceramic stirrup spout
in the form of a woman fondling
the erect penis of her partner, AD 600.

Indian influences in colonial religious art is apparent in this painting of
Christ with cross and an imaginary rendition of a Spanish city.

Double rainbow after a squall illuminates a resplendent view of Cape Horn.

Vividly painted toucan and macaw figures are among the colorful creations of Costa Rican artisans.

(Left) A waterfall in jungle setting in the Botanical Gardens of Soufrière, St Lucia.

(Below) Orchids provide a splash of glowing vermilion to the Caribbean scene.

*An Indian festival in the High Andes is a lively event with its milling throng
in brightly-colored regional costumes and distinctive headgear.*

(Left) Don Eduardo Calderón, known as "the wizard of the four winds," is one of the legendary Pacific coast curanderos who have epitomized the enduring practice of shamanism in the highland and jungle areas from Peru to Brazil.

(Below) Followers of Mahatma Gandhi add their own exotic touch to Salvador da Bahía's eclectic mix of Macumba, Catholicism and syncretic religion.

*High up in the cool hills beyond the Org mountains above Rió, the Royal Palace of Petropolis
served as a retreat from the coastal heat until Brazil's last monarch, Emperor Pedro II, abdicated in 1889.*

(Left) The Monument to the Explorers at Belém, Lisbon, commemorates the daring Portuguese adventurers who journeyed to the New World in the age of discovery.

Los Jerónimos Monastery near Lisbon stands in the point from which Vasco da Gama set sail upon his epic voyages.

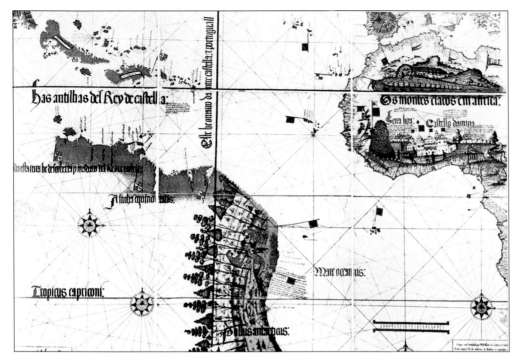

In 1494 Spanish and Portuguese ambassadors met at Tordesillas in northwestern Spain to reaffirm a line of demarcation in the mid-Atlantic previously drawn by Pope Alexander VI to divide territorial claims between the two powers. A new boundary established under the Treaty of Tordesillas (illustrated) was to enable Portugal to claim the coast of Brazil after its discovery by Cabral in 1500.

The blue and white tiles lining the cloister of São Francisco Church in Salvador da Bahía were brought from Lisbon as ballast in Portuguese ships.

CHAPTER I   Approaching South America: Caribbean Enchantment, Devil's Island and the Tikal of the Mayas

"Islands in the Stream," Ernest Hemingway called them, an evocative title conveying the sense of innocence which seems at first to pervade the West Indies: a realm of pristine enchantment, the apotheosis of nature's munificence manifested in luminous skies, indolent palms and turquoise-hued waters. This is an area blessed by brilliant light, where romance, dreams and fantasy seem to transcend the pragmatism of the material world, where relaxation is truly possible in sun-drenched paradises and where insouciance is a way of life. Their mood is exotic, their *joie de vivre* infectious, whether inspired by the pulsing beat of reggae, meringue or calypso, by the feline grace of colorful women or by the explosive power of a cricket fast bowler.

Diverse European Backgrounds

The background of Caribbean Islands is as diverse as the foreign influences that are so manifest everywhere. Britain still retains as crown colonies Anguilla, the Cayman Islands, Turks and Caicos Islands, and Montserrat, having granted independence between 1962 and 1983 to Jamaica, Trinidad and Tobago, Barbados, Guyana, the Bahamas, Grenada, Dominica, St Lucia, St Vincent Grenadines, Antigua/Barbuda and St Kitts Nevis. France, since 1946, has controlled Guadaloupe, Martinique, French Guiana and St Martin as "overseas departments," permitting their residents to be French citizens, vote in French elections and send delegates to Paris. The Netherlands administer the Netherland Antilles, consisting of Aruba, Bonaire and Curaçao in the south and, 950 kilometers to the north, the Dutch Windward Islands of St Maarten, Saba and St Eustatius.

U.S. Presence

Since the Spanish American War of 1898, the U.S. has been actively involved in the Caribbean at both the economic and military level. Today, the U.S military intervention in Grenada in 1983 and threats from communist Cuba seem part of an intangible past, as throngs of carefree tourists flock to Caribbean idylls. A formal U.S. presence is also in evidence: in Cuba, at Guantanamo Naval Base, in the Commonwealth of Puerto Rico and in the Unincorporated Territory of the Three Virgin Islands, St Thomas, St John and St Croix. They were acquired for $25 million from Denmark in 1917 to insure that strategic approaches to the Panama Canal, recently completed in 1914, would be safeguarded. It was a logical step by Washington, for as one looks at the history of the region, strategic rivalries and the role of the Caribbean as a vital transit area have traditionally been dominant factors.

Common Heritage

These islands share a common heritage. All experienced the impact of the arrival of Columbus and the fateful encounter between European and indigenous people. The

Portrait of Christopher Columbus by Rodolfo del Ghirlandaio.

successors of Columbus brought diseases and exploitation that were disastrous for the native populations, as the great Nicaraguan poet Rubén Darió poignantly observed *in El Senado del Arte*:

Sorrows, fearful occurrences, wars, feverish turmoil
This has been our unfortunate destiny
Christopher Columbus, poor admiral,
I pray for the world that you discovered.

Economics and commerce provide the thread to one of the early facets endowing the islands with a common heritage. Inca and Aztec gold fueled the transfer to Europe of vast sums of unearned income, and it was through the Caribbean that the precious metal was shipped. The West Indies thus witnessed an unfolding drama as a motley crew of pirates, buccaneers, corsairs and privateers—men like Henry Morgan and Blackbeard, whose Tower still stands on a hillside slope of the Virgin Islands' Charlotte Amalie, preyed upon the great fleets of Spanish galleons which, twice a year, sailed for Spain from Colombia, Panama and Mexico.

Other forms of commerce affected the Caribbean. Each island, to one degree or another, became scenarios for agricultural exploitation, first in cotton and tobacco, and then in sugar cane. And, as strategic rivalries unfolded, European colonial powers sent young officers like Horatio Nelson, later to be the famed admiral and victor of the battle of Trafalgar, to represent their national interests.

Sir Henry Morgan (1635–1688), most famous of the buccaneers who preyed upon the West Indian colonies of Spain in the 17th century. Knighted by King Charles II, he was appointed deputy British governor of Jamaica and died a rich and respected landowner there.

Military Memorabilia

The Caribbean is replete with monuments, statues, fortresses and cannon emplacements which testify to this turbulent past—in St Kitts, Brimstone Fortress; in the Virgin Islands' St Croix, Fort St Christian; in Guadaloupe the formidable Fort Delgres; and in Barbados, Gun Hill signal station. With the sword came the cross, in the form of competing religions. The French endowed St Lucia's Castries and Soufrière, as well as St Kitts Nevis' Basseterre, with handsome cathedrals and churches; the British graced Trinidad's Port-of-Spain with a fine Anglican Cathedral and built pleasant rural parish churches in the tranquil Barbados countryside. In Willemstad, Mikve Emanuel Israel, together with the Jewish reform temple, testifies to a felicitous rooting of Judaism amid traditional Dutch tolerance. The absence of religious strife in the Caribbean, in fact, is one of the area's endearing aspects.

Colonial Legacies

The British colonial legacy is especially noticeable. It encompasses

Admiral Horatio Nelson (1758–1805) won crucial victories for Britain in the wars with Napoleonic France during a distinguished naval career that had included duty as a young officer in the West Indies.

traditions as diverse as political pluralism, reflected in parliamentary buildings and judicial systems, formulation of free speech and human rights (in Port-of-Spain's Woodford Square, and in the Trinidadian national anthem), in cricket, a game that arouses national passions, and in the Victorian Gothic architecture of buildings with evocative names like Queen's Royal College.

European architecture is evident, too, in the waterfront houses of Curaçao's capital of Willemstad, which are unabashedly Dutch, while the Hôtel de Ville in Guadaloupe's capital Point-à-Pitre has an unmistakably Gallic charm.

Sugar Trade and "Cutlass Profit"

After tobacco, cotton and rum, it was sugar cane that became the great income producer. Ships plying the "triangular trade" brought slaves from Africa to provide the needed plantation labor, and carried West Indian products, primarily sugar, back to the Old World. The Bajan poet Edward Braithwaite tells us that

The explosive grace of a fast bowler epitomizes West Indians' passionate love of cricket, one of the British empire's most enduring legacies.

> The islands roared into green plantations
> ruled by silver sugar cane
> sweat and profit
> cutlass profit
> islands ruled by sugar cane.

Slaves who escaped hid in the jungles and mountains of Dominica, arguably the wildest and most beautiful of all the Caribbean islands. These "Maroons" came to symbolize the desire for liberty that would fuel early 19th-century revolts in Haiti and Guadaloupe and would, 150 years later, provide the theme for Carpentier's great literary oeuvre *El Reino de este Mundo* (*The Kingdom of this World*). It would also stimulate a remarkable Jamaican, Marcus Garvey, to articulate these feeling in the United Negro Improvement Association (UNIA), in the early 20th century.

Defining a Caribbean Identity

It is against this polyglot colonial background that the Caribbean has struggled to forge its own identity: a difficult task for islands whose dependence upon primary products and tourism makes them susceptible to the whims of international markets. Yet the Caribbean does have a distinct identity, manifested through such musical figures as the Mighty Sparrow, the words of whose songs contain moral messages; such painters of an authentic surrealism that is inspired by the jungle vegetation and mystical rituals of his native Cuba as Wifredo Lam; and such literary figures as the St Lucian Nobel Prize winner Derek Walcott. His *Omeros*, a remarkable work of 8,000 lines of poetry peopled by Caribbean personages with Greek names, displays an unbridled lavishness of alliteration and metaphor evocative of the Caribbean. He explains the title *Omeros*:

> . . . and *O* was the conch shell's invocation, *mer* was
> both mother and sea in our Antillean patois,
> *os* a grey bone, and the white surf as it crashes
> and spreads its sibilant collar on a lace shore.

Shells, surf, the sea . . . this is what the Caribbean is all about, the pink and white shells displayed on the

Caribbean girl with maracas and a fruit bowl.

Basseterre waterfront as apt an icon of life in these idyllic climes as are the buoyant orchids or a waterfall in a botanical garden. No wonder Columbus, and those who followed, stayed in the New World, unlike the Vikings for whom, five centuries before, the visit to Newfoundland's inhospitable L'Anse aux Meadows had been short-lived. The Caribbean seemingly offered everything to the early Europeans, otherwise accustomed as they had been to a limited range of foods, inclement weather, and stereotyped socio-political regimes. Here was a new sense of freedom, of glorious weather, strange flora and fauna, majestic topography, provocative women, easily exploitable workers, and always the prospects of gold and untold riches.

There was also something else: manifestations of a marvelous reality. Did not Columbus, probably sighting playful manatees near Santo Domingo, believe that he had stumbled upon what Muller-Bergh suggests were the legendary carnivorous sirens, half female and half fish, who used their bewitching voices to lure sailors to their death?

One can imagine the excitement of those hardened European adventurers, intrepid figures who epitomized the age of discovery in the 15th and 16th centuries, when they arrived in the Caribbean. Nothing pays greater tribute to them than an immense monument on the Tagus River, five kilometers before arriving at the heart of Lisbon. Close by, the magnificent Los Jerónimos Monastery stands near the point from which Vasco da Gama embarked upon his epic voyages. Many of these heroic personages would leave their mark, not only on the Caribbean, but on the Americas: it is to Amerigo Vespucci that the continent owes its name, and for Magellan that the strait joining the Atlantic and Pacific in southern South America is named. As in the case of South America, the political, economic, religious and cultural ties binding the Old World to the New World would persist for centuries thereafter and, to a certain degree, still do today.

Le Bagne: The Extraordinary French Penal Colony of Guiana

In the late 18th century, a different brand of European would come to the Caribbean, in very different circumstances from the earlier arrivals. These were political undesirables like Billaud-Varenne and Collot d'Herbois who, after the French Revolution of 1789, were dispatched as prisoners to the fetid jungles of French Guiana, on the north coast of South America. It would be here, in mainland camps and on three offshore islands, that Le Bagne, or French penal colony, would develop.

Florentine merchant and navigator Amerigo Vespucci, who gave his name to the New World.

Alfred Dreyfus, a young French Jewish artillery officer, was unjustly condemned to Devil's Island in the 1890s for allegedly giving the Germans military secrets. His case polarized the nation until his vindication brought release, after five years of imprisonment, in 1906.

Captain Dreyfus on L'Ile du Diable (Devil's Island)

Between the 1790s and the early 1940s, when Le Bagne was closed, it received close to 70,000 unfortunates, who varied from murderers and felons to political prisoners. The most famous of the latter was a young French Jewish army captain, Alfred Dreyfus, who was unjustly accused of giving military secrets to Germany. He spent five years on Devil's Island in the 1890s, his case polarizing France between the army general staff and anti-semitic conservatives who victimized him, and the liberals who championed his cause, like the writer Emile Zola.

Devil's Island, where the few political prisoners were housed, was actually the most pleasant of the penal colony's three offshore islands, ironically called Les Isles de Salut, or Islands of Health, because of the welcome offshore breezes. The other two islands were Ile St Joseph, now a rest and recuperation center for the French Foreign Legion, but once the place where especially recalcitrant prisoners were subjected to solitary confinement in infamous underground pits; and Ile Royale, where up to 700 prisoners were incarcerated. The present ruined buildings, scene of their detention, are a somber reminder of a bizarre and often fantastic past, filled with lurid romances between convicts and officials' wives, of frightening homosexual violence and of guillotinings under a relentless tropical sun.

Franz Kafka's *The Penal Colony*

Ile Royale, 250 meters away from Devil's Island across shark-infested waters, is the only island open to visitors. It has a "swimming pool" along the shore, a church decorated by a convict artist, a group of prison installations and a small cemetery. It is a strange sensation to walk around, and to be reminded of how so many horrors could have transpired in such a bucolic setting. Perhaps only *The Penal Colony*, a terrifying short story by the brilliant 20th-century writer Franz Kafka, effectively conjures up the reality of this extraordinary place.

Tikal

If one approaches South America by sailing down the west coast from North America, Mexico and Central America, a stop at the port of Puerto Quetzal enables one to visit a site which embodies the marvelous reality of the Americas—the Mayan site of Tikal in Guatemala.

The 576-square-kilometer site shows evidence of 1,700 years of occupation, from 800 BC to AD 900, the latter the time of the Late Classic Maya Period. The site is representative of the notable cultural, artistic, architectural, mathematical, astronomical, agricultural and commercial achievements of the Mayas, as well as of their advanced sense of urban planning. This is particularly in evidence in the Great Plaza, where the triangular tiered Pyramids of the Great Jaguar and the Masks, and the complex of buildings comprising the North and Central Acropolis, are the most dramatic aspects.

Tikal symbolizes the brilliant engineering and architectural feats of ancient peoples in the remote past. In our century, nothing has eclipsed another extraordinary accomplishment, in a geographical location not far distant from Tikal. This was the incredible Canal that was constructed across the Isthmus of Panama between 1904 and 1914.

The waterfront "Careenage" and the Assembly Building in Bridgetown, capital of Barbados.

The statue of the English admiral, Lord Nelson, in Bridgetown is a reminder of 18th- and 19th-century colonial rivalries in the Caribbean.

Gun Hill Tower signal station, overlooking sugar fields in the Barbados countryside, is maintained by the Barbados National Trust.

In a tranquil setting redolent of the English countryside, St John's Church symbolizes the Anglican religious tradition.

(Above) The hilltop location of St John's Church offers a magnificent panoramic view of the Barbados countryside and coast.

(Below) En route to Scott's Head, the village of Sufrie nestling below mountain peaks amid exuberant tropical foliage shows an aspect of the unique charm of Dominica, once the haunt of escaped slaves and now perhaps the most beautiful of the Caribbean islands.

Statue of the remarkable Marcus Garvey, early 20th-century protagonist of the United Negro Improvement Association, near Ocho Rios, Jamaica.

NATIONAL ANTHEM
OF
TRINIDAD AND TOBAGO

FORGED FROM THE LOVE OF LIBERTY
IN THE FIRES OF HOPE AND PRAYER.
WITH BOUNDLESS FAITH IN OUR DESTINY
WE SOLEMNLY DECLARE.
SIDE BY SIDE WE STAND.
ISLANDS OF THE BLUE CARIBBEAN SEA
THIS OUR NATIVE LAND.
WE PLEDGE OUR LIVES TO THEE.

HERE EVERY CREED AND RACE
FIND AN EQUAL PLACE.
AND MAY GOD BLESS OUR NATION.

HERE EVERY CREED AND RACE
FIND AN EQUAL PLACE
AND MAY GOD BLESS OUR NATION.

*(Above) Outside the Red House, which faces the central square in Port-of-Spain, a plaque with
Trinidad's national anthem proudly hails the island's commitment to ensure that "every creed and race find an equal place."*

*(Below) The Red House is the site of Trinidad's Parliament.
It was originally painted red in 1897 to celebrate Queen Victoria's diamond jubilee.*

Seigneurial Roomor, next to the Archbishop's residence, is an example of Port-of-Spain's magnificent turn-of-the-century architecture that evokes an era of sugar barons and British colonial rule.

With pointed arched windows, striking tower and brick facade, Queens Royal College, built in 1904, testifies to Port-of-Spain's claim to possessing the Caribbean's most imposing Victorian Gothic architecture.

Decorative clocktower in Basseterre's central square commemorates an esteemed scion of the island, Thomas Berkeley.

The somber presence of a cannon dominating a superb coastal vista testifies to the often turbulent past of St Kitts in European power struggles for colonial hegemony in the Caribbean.

The entrance to St Kitts' Brimstone Hill Fortress, where British troops mounted the first cannons in 1690.

A handsome church overlooking a park in Castries, capital of St Lucia. With a large Catholic community, the city is named after French colonial minister de Castries, governor of the island in 1784.

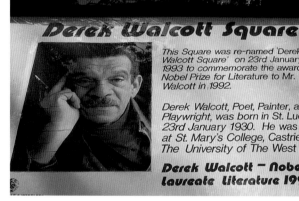

Sign at the entrance to Derek Walcott Square in Castries honors St Lucia's famed Nobel Prize-winning poet.

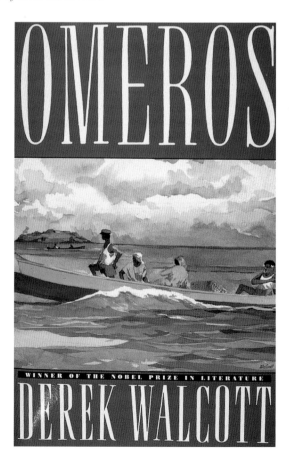

Omeros by Derek Walcott is a contemporary odyssey in a Caribbean setting, a work distinguished by rich descriptive metaphors and intriguing characters endowed with Homeric names.

Majestic Gros and Petit Pitons soar above St Lucia's picturesque port of Soufrière.

Billowing clouds over a St Lucia seaside village aglow in late afternoon sunlight.

This graceful church overlooks Soufrière's main square, Place Principale, a name which evokes the French presence on the island until England gained control in 1814.

Volcano and La Soufrière sulphur springs.

Streetside board at Charlotte Amalie pronounces that having three or four wives is philosophically unconstitutional!

Statue honoring teacher Edith Williams in Charlotte Amalie, capital of the three islands of St Thomas, St Johns and St Croix that comprise the U.S. Virgin Islands.

In St Thomas, the sweeping bay of Charlotte Amalie accommodates small seagoing vessels as well as large liners.

(Above) The red-roofed, turquoise colored Legislature Building in its delightful garden setting.

(Right) A line of cannons at St Croix's Fort St Christian evokes a colorful colonial past, which includes the U.S purchase of the Virgin Islands from Denmark in 1917 for $25 million.

(Below) In Charlotte Amalie, Blackbeard's Tower harks back to the lawless days when pirates terrorized both Spanish treasure galleons and defenseless merchantmen.

Seen from the Otra Banda side of Curaçao's capital of Willemstad, the old waterfront houses of the Punda mirror the Amsterdam canal architecture of the island's Dutch settlers.

Willemstad's Mikve-Emanuel Israel, oldest synagogue in the New World.

A patio at the Mikve-Emanuel Israel Synagogue provides a restful area for contemplation.

In Guadeloupe's capital of Point-à-Pitre, the statue of French General Frébault looks out over the charming Place de la Victoire.

The former home of St Jean Perse in Point-à-Pitre is now a museum dedicated to the French writer's life and work.

The Hôtel de Ville or Town Hall unequivocally proclaims Guadeloupe's French connection. In the early 1800s the island was the scene of a heroic anti-slavery revolt against Napoleonic rule and was briefly occupied by the British, but it was restored to France in 1816.

View of Devil's Island from Ile Royale. A penal colony was established in French Guiana on the north coast of South America in the late 18th century. Devil's Island was actually the least insalubrious of the penal colony's three offshore islands.

Poignant reminder of the heavy toll tropical diseases took on the settlers: the children's cemetery on Ile Royale.

A tombstone at the children's cemetery.

The old convict church on Ile Royale.

Ghostly ruins evoke phantoms of the past on Ile Royale, where up to 700 prisoners could be accommodated at any one time.

Famed tiered pyramid Temple I (Temple of the Great Jaguar) and Temple II (Temple of the Masks), similar in structure and 38 meters in height, were built about AD 700 by the ruler Ah Cacao. Examples of Mayan architectural genius, they close off respectively the east and west sides of the Great Plaza at the Mayan site of Tikal in Guatemala.

(Right) A somber Rain God presides over his domain in the lush jungle foliage of Tikal.

(Below) Around the Great Plaza of Tikal, to the north and south, and surrounded by jungle, are the North Acropolis and Central Acropolis, with palace-type ceremonial buildings and a stone statue of the Mayan rain deity.

CHAPTER II How the Builders of the Panama Canal Created the World's Eighth Wonder

The End of An Era: December 31, 1999

On December 31, 1999, four months after Panama's first woman President, Mireya Moscoso, assumed office, the United States relinquished its control over the Panama Canal and all training areas and bases in Panama. The handover brought to an end an extraordinary era, during which about 830,000 ships passed through the Canal since it opened in 1914. For the U.S., the saga of the Canal began in 1903, with a remarkable treaty between the United States and a Panama that had suddenly become independent after being under Colombian control.

The treaty signed by U.S. Secretary of State Hay and Philippe Bunau-Varilla was as fantastic as would be the extraordinary canal that was subsequently constructed. The prelude to the treaty was a colorful one. Bunau-Varilla was a French engineer who had worked on the canal during the ill-fated attempt of the Compagnie Universelle du Canal Interocéanique, under the direction of Ferdinand de Lesseps between 1882 and 1887, to build a canal across the Panama Isthmus. In early 1903 he made contact with Dr Manuel Guerrero Amador, the representative of a nascent Panamanian independence movement, thereby setting in motion a complex pattern of diplomatic intrigues.

Bunau-Varilla subsequently met with President Theodore Roosevelt, primarily to gain assurances that the U.S. would not intervene on behalf of Colombia if Panama sought to gain independence. Roosevelt had become interested in the concept of a canal after realizing how long it took U.S. warships to reach Cuba from Hawaii by traveling via Cape Horn at the time of the 1898 Spanish American War. Thus the decisive appearance of the gunboat *Nashville* in Colón Harbor in 1903, at precisely the moment of a Panamanian uprising against Colombia, was perhaps more than coincidental!

Terms of the Treaty Between Hay and Bunau-Varilla

The way was now open for the signing of the November 18, 1903 Treaty in which, remarkably, the Frenchman Bunau-Varilla had contrived to have himself designated as the representative of the newly independent Panama. The Treaty authorized the United States to build a canal through an area that was ten miles wide, which would be a sovereign U.S. Zone in perpetuity. (This area was known as the Canal Zone until 1977, when its status was revised by the Carter/Torrijos Treaties.) In return, the United States guaranteed the independence of Panama, as well as the payment to Panama of $10 million upon ratification, and an annuity of $250,000 payable from 1912 on.

Thus began a fantastic adventure. It was truly an incredible feat of engineering, a rival for any of the world's great wonders in imagination and implementation. For the author, who made frequent visits to the U.S. Southern Military Command (SOUTHCOM) during his years of military/diplomatic assignments in South America from 1969 to 1976, the Canal and its incredible background never ceased to be a source of awe. The U.S. achievement in successfully completing the Canal in 1904–1914 can be even more readily appreciated when set against the disastrous French failure of the Compagnie Universelle du Canal Interocéanique to build a canal across the Isthmus of Panama in the 1880s.

French Débâcle in the 1880s

The French had failed because of their obdurate refusal to modify an initially ill-conceived plan. Ferdinand de Lesseps, the brilliant and daring entrepreneur who had, against all odds, built and opened the Suez Canal in 1869, was convinced that in Panama he could construct a ground-level canal without locks, just as he had done in Egypt's desert sands. However, de Lesseps never really grasped the impact of Panama's rugged mountainous terrain, the dank heat which induced malaria and yellow fever, and the westerly flowing Chagres River, whose raging torrent during the rainy season would inevitably overflow into and inundate any prospective north/south canal route.

In 1887, after five frustrating years in which 20,000 lives had been expended in progressing a paltry 18 kilometers, La Compagnie Universelle virtually abandoned the project. Mismanagement, ill-advised planning, release of fraudulent information to the public to raise new funds, payment of bribes to influential Congressional deputies and huge losses suffered by hundreds of thousands of small investors who had believed in de Lesseps, triggered what was the world's first major international financial scandal. The outcome was the 1892 suicide of the prominent financier Baron Jacques de Reinach, embarrassing trials for company executives and, later in 1894, the formation of a new company—La Compagnie Nouvelle de Panama.

Between 1907 and 1914, the years in which the U.S. Military was responsible for completing construction of the Panama Canal, four officers rendered outstanding service.
Under the overall leadership of Colonel Goethals, Colonel Sibert supervised the Gatún Dam; Colonel Gaillard dug through the mountain terrain to create the Gaillard (Culebra) Cut and Colonel Gorgas directed the medical facilities.

Four Major Factors in U.S. Canal Construction

The Compagnie Nouvelle did very little in the ensuing ten years, and in 1904 the U.S. purchased its rights, property and equipment for $40 million. Thus, with the Hay/Bunau-Varilla Treaty signed, the U.S., under the initial able leadership of civilian engineer John F. Stevens from 1904 to 1907, embarked upon the project which the U.S. Military would complete between 1907 and 1914.

The U.S. succeeded because four major steps were taken to avoid the problems that had plagued the French. The first was the adoption of a series of vitally important technological and engineering innovations. These included the establishment of an elaborate system of lock complexes; the damming of the Chagres River by the Gatún Dam and the corollary creation of the huge 163-square-mile artificial Gatún Lake; and excavation through the 312-foot high Continental Divide of a canal passage under the supervision of Colonel David DuBose Gaillard, which was initially called the Culebra Cut, and later the Gaillard Cut.

Secondly, under the able medical leadership of Colonel William C. Gorgas, steps were implemented to resolve the sanitation and health problems that had plagued the French. Drawing upon the pioneering work of Walter Reed and Ronald Ross, Gorgas—well known to military personnel for the hospital in Panama that bears his name—identified the female *stegomyia fasciata* mosquito as the source of yellow fever infection, and the female *anopheles* as the source of malaria. The organization of appropriate preventive measures was instrumental in holding deaths in the ten years of U.S. operation to about 5,000, one quarter of the toll reached under the Compagnie Universelle in a mere five years.

Thirdly, U.S. responsibility for canal construction from 1907 to 1914 under Colonel George W. Goethals and a staff of outstanding officers insured a unilateral chain of command, reliable control, efficient administration and encouragement to display initiative. Finally, the U.S. was able to deal directly with Panama, thereby obviating the political problems which the French had encountered when Panama was under Colombian jurisdiction.

Publications

The epic drama of the Panama Canal has been told in many notable works. For gripping narrative, scholarly research and compelling photographic imagery none surpasses David McCullough's brilliant 1977 publication *The Path between the Seas*, an indispensable and comprehensive source of material. Also invaluable as a pictorial reference is the fold-out publication of the Panama Canal Commission, entitled simply *The Panama Canal*. It covers succinctly and clearly the fundamental technical aspects of canal construction, and describes a typical canal transit.

Between 1904 and August 15, 1914, when the steamer *Ancón* made the first transit, the US successfully constructed a canal extending 50 miles (80 kilometers), from Atlantic to Pacific deep water. The key was the 14 spillway earthen Gatún Dam, 105 feet high, which used the water from the surging Chagres River to create an immense artificial lake with a depth of about 45 feet, below which were 40 feet of earth. The rationale for the lake was threefold. It solved the problem of the Chagres River, obviated the need for excessive excavation in the troublesome rocky terrain of the Continental Divide and defused problems implicit in tidal height differentials of about 20 feet on the Pacific side, and a mere three feet on the Atlantic side.

Panama Canal Operational Aspects

The Canal functions today in virtually the same manner as when it was completed in 1914. Each of the six locks has the dual capacity to handle simultaneously two ships, going in either the same or in opposite directions. On the Atlantic side, the three locks comprising the Gatún Lock Complex raise or lower a ship a total of 85 feet, each lock accounting for just over 28 feet. On the Pacific side, there are two lock complexes, separated by the one-mile long man-made Miraflores Lake: first the Pedro Miguel Lock, which raises or lowers a ship 31 feet, and then the two locks of the Miraflores Complex, which each raises or lowers a ship 27 feet, making a total of 54 feet.

Prior to entering the Canal, a ship must take on at least one Panama canal pilot. The ship then proceeds south from Limón Bay, past the breakwaters between the port of Cristobal and the town of Colón, towards Gatún Locks. At Buoy 16 to the right, the narrow entrance to the ill-fated canal dug by the French can be observed.

Phenomenal Water Consumption

Each of the three twin Gatún Lock chambers possesses the uniform dimensions of all chambers on the canal: a length of 1,000 feet, and a width of 110 feet. Amazingly, these chambers are filled or emptied entirely by the force of gravity,

Panama Canal Cross Section

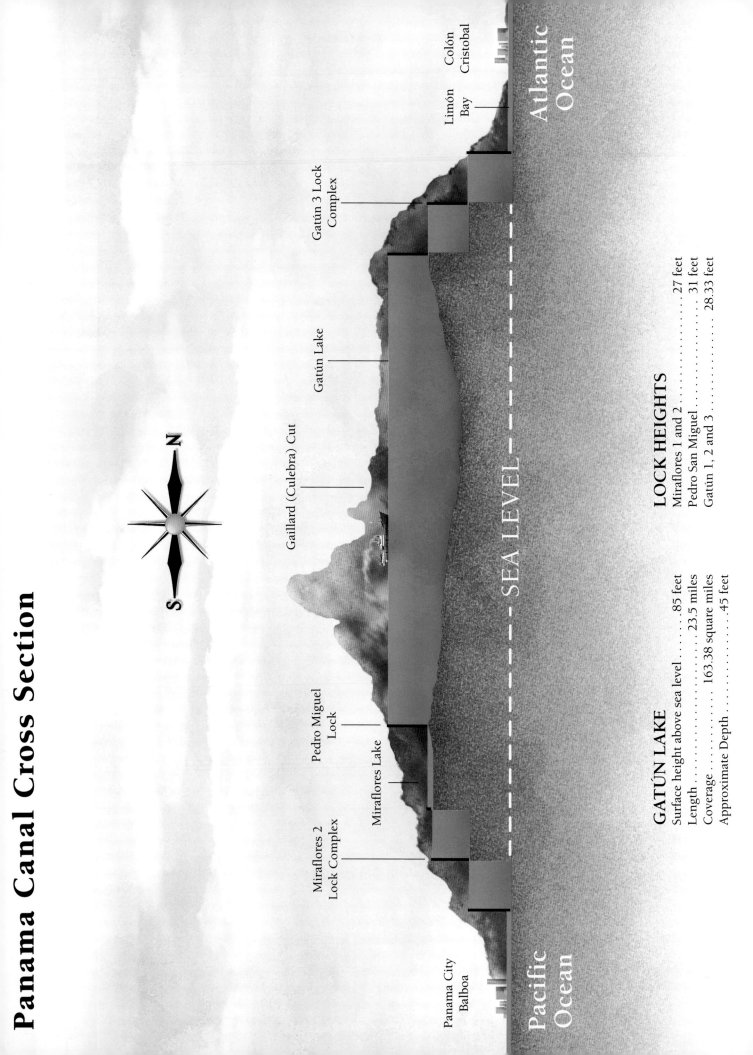

Limón
Bay
Colón
Cristobal

Atlantic
Ocean

Gatún 3 Lock
Complex

Gatún Lake

Gaillard (Culebra) Cut

SEA LEVEL

N
S

Pedro Miguel
Lock

Miraflores Lake

Miraflores 2
Lock Complex

Panama City
Balboa

Pacific
Ocean

GATÚN LAKE

Surface height above sea level . . . . . .85 feet
Length . . . . .23.5 miles
Coverage . . . . 163.38 square miles
Approximate Depth . . . . .45 feet

LOCK HEIGHTS

Miraflores 1 and 2 . . . . .27 feet
Pedro San Miguel . . . . 31 feet
Gatún 1, 2 and 3 . . . . 28.33 feet

without the use of any pumps! The amount of water employed in lowering or raising a ship during a single transit is truly phenomenal: about 52 million gallons of fresh water. Since about 33 ships transit daily, their total 1.5 billion gallons of water consumption is roughly equivalent to that used daily by the Netherlands' 15 million people!

Three Vitally Important Components

Each lock complex has three vital components. The first component is the main and auxiliary lock gates, each of which is about seven feet thick, weighs 690 tons and is as high as a seven-story building. Secondly, two huge 18-foot diameter tunnels, parallel to each other and linked by 21 culverts, provide the water which fills a chamber in about eight minutes. Finally, the 55 ton "mules," or electronically powered mobile machines, have towing cables which can pull up to 70,000 pounds (35 tons).

Panama Canal Transit

After being raised a total of 85 feet by the three Gatún Locks, a ship enters Gatún Lake. Immediately to the right is the building housing the offices, equipment and personnel responsible for security, fire control and implementation of the Vessel Emergency Reaction Plan. Just beyond, the top of Gatún Dam can be faintly glimpsed in the distance.

The ship now sails the 23 1/2 miles south through Gatún Lake, passing on the left the point where the Chagres River flows into the Canal at Gamboa. From the ship, one cannot see a second major dam, the Madden Dam, which was constructed in the 1930s near the source of the Chagres at an altitude of 265 feet above sea level. The ship now enters the Gaillard Cut, known for its devastating landslides and their corollary loss of life during the years of construction. Shortly before reaching the Pedro Miguel Lock, the ship passes on the left Gold Hill, whose 587-foot elevation makes it the highest promontory along the channel. Contractor's Hill, almost directly opposite, has a 370-foot high elevation.

This part of the transit is the most spectacular, the view enlivened by the striking tropical vegetation and by the occasionally nonchalant alligator that swims the 500 feet across the Canal. Originally excavated to a width of 300 feet, the Gaillard Cut has been progressively widened since the 1930s so that most of it now has an additional 200 feet of width.

Pedro Miguel and Miraflores Locks

The Pacific-bound ship enters Pedro Miguel Locks, which are just under one mile in length, at the southern end of the Gaillard Cut. After being lowered 31 feet and crossing the one-mile long Miraflores Lake, the ship arrives at Miraflores Locks, which are slightly over one mile in length, and whose lock gates are the tallest of any in the system, as a result of the extreme tidal variation in the Pacific Ocean. From here there is an excellent view of Fort Clayton which was, until December 31, 1999, a characteristically visible symbol of U.S. military presence in Panama.

Once a ship has been lowered the additional 54 feet through the two Miraflores Locks, it is at sea level. It is now on the final phase of the transit, en route to Balboa harbor, whose lively atmosphere may be brightened by the arrival of such colorful vessels as the *Cauhtemoc*, the training ship for cadets in the Mexican Navy. Beyond lies the soaring Bridge of the Americas, with Balboa to the immediate left and behind Panama City.

Panama Control Commission

The visitor to Balboa's Ancón Hill will find the Panama Control Commission building ensconced amid exuberant foliage and looking down to the monument honoring Colonel George Goethals. The Commission, a U.S. Government agency, began operating on October 1, 1979; it came into being to replace the former Panama Canal Company and to oversee the 20-year transition until full Panamanian control on December 31, 1999. Its establishment followed the signing of the two treaties by Presidents Carter and Torrijos, and their subsequent approval in Panama by a plebiscite in October 1977, and in the U.S. by Senate ratification in 1978. From 1979 to 1990, the Administrator in charge was North American, and from 1990 on Panamanian.

The 1977 and 1979 Treaties

The two treaties, entitled the Panama Canal Treaty and the Treaty on the Permanent Neutrality and Operation of the Canal, contained four main stipulations, of which the fourth is critical in terms of U.S. national security:

1. The U.S. would operate the Canal until 2000, when U.S. control of all bases and training areas would cease.
2. Between 1979 and 2000 the U.S. with the participation of the Panama defense forces, was to be responsible for the defense of the Canal.
3. Effective in 1979, Panama was to have jurisdiction over the Canal Zone, an area extending for five miles on each side of the Canal.
4. After January 1, 2000, the U.S. would retain perpetual authority to protect and defend the Canal in the event of threats to the neutrality of the Canal.

The two decades since the signing of the Treaties generally proceeded smoothly, as transfer to Panama or to a newly coordinated administration of complete facilities or parts thereof (Ft Amador, Ft Gulick, Ft Sherman, Ft Clayton Training Grounds, *et al*) went into effect. During this period, the U.S. retained control of such defense facilities as Albrook Air Station, Ft Clayton (except the training area), Rodman U.S. Naval Station, and others.

A serious crisis occurred in 1989, when U.S. military forces executed "Operation Just Cause." Its objective was to oust Panamanian strongman Manuel Noriega, accused of unsavory machinations in drug dealing, of the brutal murder of political adversary Dr Hugo Spadafora and of the sale of arms to leftist guerrilla terrorists in Nicaragua and Colombia.

Implications and Questions

The December 31, 1999 handover of the Canal to Panama has inevitably raised questions. Contemporary air mobility has lessened the strategic significance of the Canal, and the Treaties affirm the U.S. right to intervene militarily in event of threats to the Canal's neutrality. However, for commercial ships, like those traveling from Nagasaki to New York which save 3,000 miles by using the Canal rather than rounding South America's southern tip, questions arise: will the former non-profit structure of the Canal be changed, with profits not being reinvested in Panamanian infrastructure? Will tolls be raised from a current average of $34,000, or around $70,000 for the largest ships? And what, if any, will be the implications of the contract which Panama signed in 1997, to grant Hong Kong-based company Hutchison Whampoa Ltd a 25-year contract to run the port terminal at each end of the Canal? Finally, will the endemic violence of lawless Colombian rebels spill over into Panamanian territory and, if so, how will the 13,000-man National Police act to contain them?

Perhaps such questions are in keeping with what has been a tortuous and difficult chapter in the history of the Americas. Few, if any, engineering feats are likely to rival the remarkable building of the Panama Canal, surely the eighth Wonder of the World and one destined to take its place forever in the pantheon of Latin America's marvelous realities.

Monument to Colonel Goethals in front of the Panama Control Commission building in Colón.

Red roofs at a base built after the U.S. military completed the Canal in 1914; in accordance with the 1977 Carter/Torrijos Treaties, the Canal reverted to Panamanian control on December 31, 1999.

Canal lock shows two chambers —with different water levels— which are capable of simultaneously accommodating two ships.

(Below) At Gatún Locks, as tall as a seven-storey building, main and auxiliary gates, each seven feet thick and 690 tons in weight, open mechanically in two minutes.

*The Mexican cadet tall ship Cauhtemoc at anchor in Balboa harbor is one of
several traditional seagoing vessels used to train future Mexican naval officers.*

CHAPTER III Peru, Land of Pre-Columbian Marvels and Viceregal Splendors

A dramatic moment, tinged with anticipation—arrival in Callao, Lima's sprawling sea port. For this is the gateway to a fabled pre-Hispanic past that conjures up visions of kings crowned with lavish plumes, of shirts glittering with gold plaques, of *chasqui* long-distance couriers and of *quipus* recording complex statistics on knotted cords, of remarkably advanced social, political and economic systems, and of an Inca empire which between 1430 and 1532 held sway over approximately 15 million people.

How can we not be mesmerized by people who accomplished so much with so little? The ancient Peruvians had no wheel, no arch, no major river system and no significant areas of arable land. Nor did they have animals to transport humans, for the camelid family of vicuñas, guanacos, alpacas and llamas will carry only objects as cargo. Finally, isolated as they were, these ancient Andean peoples possessed none of the benefits which usually result from the interchange of ideas with other civilizations. Peru today is fascinating at many levels; but the stunning feats and sense of aesthetics of the ancient pre-Hispanic peoples, the greatest of South America, make other accomplishments pale by comparison.

Pizarro's Conquest: Fantastic Reality

The 1532 conquest of the Inca Atahualpa's vast empire by a handful of Spaniards under the ruthless conquistador

Francisco Pizarro adds another chapter to the fantastic reality of South America. Onto the pre-Hispanic polytheism and hierarchic political rule of the Inca, the Spaniards superimposed a Catholic monotheism and an equally hierarchic form of government, that of the Spanish sovereign. The result of the Spanish presence in South America would be, from 1550 until independence was achieved in 1820, what we know as the Age of the Viceroys, the governing emissaries of the Spanish king in the New World. Their major legacies were authoritarianism, religious architecture and colonial art.

Both to the north and south of Lima stretches the arid, narrow Pacific desert coast. Bisected by sporadic river valleys, its total length is almost 2,400 kilometers from the northern border with Ecuador to the southern frontier with Chile. To the east, the peaks of the mighty Cordillera of the Andes soar above 20,000 feet. Beyond lie the tropical, dank and often mephitic Amazonian jungle lowlands that cover almost 60 per cent of Peru's territory.

Woman of Cuzco: almond eyes, high cheekbones, olive complexion and sleek jet-black hair hark back to a bygone past and to the possible Asiatic origins of such indigenous peoples of the High Andes as the Quechua and the Aymara.

None of this terrain is particularly conducive to notable cultural accomplishments and, indeed, the tropical lowlands have bequeathed nothing of significance to posterity. But the highlands and the coast are another matter. We tend to think immediately of the Incas, who controlled an area stretching from Colombia and Ecuador as far south as Argentina and Chile, where the Mapuches were their inveterate enemies. Yet, astoundingly, there were more than ten major cultures which preceded the Incas and which, from 500 BC on, bequeathed to posterity a galaxy of scintillating achievements in textiles, feather ornamentation, gold and silver objects, adobe constructions, stone and wood carvings and socio-political organization.

In remote areas, some of the ancient religious rituals still persist; and, in the Urubamba Valley area around Cuzco, distinctive clothing of brilliant colors and unusual shapes are a reminder of this impressive past. Since the ancient Peruvians left no written material, knowledge of their past comes to us from myths, legends, archaeological evidence and especially from such Spanish chroniclers as Garcilaso de la Vega, whose house still stands in Cuzco. Their world, relived today in costume, jewelry, festivals and religious rites, is one of the greatest marvels of South America.

Alexander von Humboldt (1769–1859) identified the cold Pacific current that bears his name. Born in Berlin, von Humboldt was typical of the new breed of naturalists, archaeologists and explorers who came to South America in the 19th century to "rediscover" the continent—not to search for gold but to examine scientifically its natural and man-made wonders.

Pristine Preservation and Conservation

Their heritage is dazzling and much of it remains in a pristine state because of a combination of felicitous factors. The Peruvian and northern Chilean coast, one of the world's driest areas, receives virtually no rain owing to the presence of the Andes to the east and the cold current to the west—a current first identified by the early 19th-century naturalist Alexander von Humboldt. A *garúa* mist intrudes in winter, but the only rain comes with the periodic Niño current. What this means is that above-ground structures like ancient temples and adobe buildings, earth designs, and below-ground tombs have survived remarkably well for some 2,000 years. So too have the dazzling treasures from Peru's ten major highland and coastal cultures.

Highland and Pre-Columbian Cultures

The first of the four dynamic highland Andean peoples, whose influence in all cases expanded to the coast, was Chavín de Huantar, in northern Peru. A theocratic and pan-Peruvian unifier, this group is famed for its incised stone carvings and powerful ceramics executed between about 800 BC to AD 100. A related coastal culture, that of Sechin, created the only stone temple with designs in South America. Its poignant and often frightening imagery, including blinded victims with shredded tongues, is a 3,000-year-old lament to the horrors of war as moving as is Pablo Picasso's painting of the destruction of Guérnica in the Spanish Civil War.

The other major highland cultures were centered in southern Peru, and on the steppe-like Altiplano of what is now Bolivia. These were the Tihuanaco and Wari cultures, from about AD 300–1000, and the Incas, whose period of hegemony was from about 1430 to 1532.

The Incas 1430-1532

Inca accomplishments epitomize what the marvelous reality of South America is all about. Here was a dynamic, technically skilled and culturally inspired people who also organized a formidable socio-economic system among its estimated 15 million subjects. These members of the Tawantinsuyu, or Four Corners of the Universe, governed from Cuzco, in the southern Peruvian highlands.

Virtually everyone in the Inca state worked, and everyone was provided for. Under the *ayllu* system a *chacra*, or small parcel of land of about two acres, was allotted annually to each married head of household, who also received a state allotment of llamas and basic clothing. The produce from his *chacra* was used, firstly, to make "contributions"— the equivalent of modern tax payments—to the Inca ruler, the Sun Deity's *amautu* priests and local chiefs called *caciques*. Secondly, it provided his own family with subsistence, with perhaps a small surplus left over for barter in local markets. Finally, it furnished support to such needy people as elderly widows, the mentally handicapped and injured veterans.

This system of agrarian collectivism, a precursor of the 20th-century Soviet communist collective farm system, appears to have worked much better! The Incas also displayed ruling tendencies approximating what we know in the 20th century as fascism. The Inca, or supreme ruler, effectively ran a tightly controlled, elitist, and perpetuating dictatorship, with rigid regulations enforced by brutal punishments. But there was a rationale behind these authoritarian controls, as one example illustrates. The law forbidding subjects of the *hatunruna*, or common people, to move from one village to another, for example, was designed not only as a control to keep track of subjects, but also to insure their well being. Population census details told the government exactly how much corn, *chuñu* dried potato and other products needed to be locally stockpiled in case of emergencies. The authorities had the prescience to realize that arbitrary population movements would clearly disrupt this organized planning, with detrimental consequences for the populace.

Sacsahuayman and Machu Picchu

The Incas were a pragmatic, highly organized people, and this is reflected in their constructivist designs, in which pictographs are placed inside squares in logical sequence. Order and administration were what the Incas were all about, and nothing shows that better than their impressive engineering and architectural ingenuity. They built rope bridges over ravines, 16,000 kilometers of road network, irrigation terracing along Andean slopes, as well as some quite astonishing edifices.

Using only primitive tools, they shaped, transported and erected immense 200-ton stone blocks with such consummate precision that the proverbial razor blade will not fit between them. Thus a fortress-type structure like Sacsahuayman, a mighty three-tiered terraced complex of three 100-meter-long stone-block walls, is astonishing by any standards.

The "Lost City" of Machu Picchu

Eighty kilometers away by winding train through the Urubamba Valley is Machu Picchu, the best known of all the

Inca sites. And rightly so. Its location at an altitude of 8,800 feet, high above the Urubamba River and surrounded by majestic peaks, is as breathtaking now as it must have appeared to the North American Hiram Bingham, who discovered Machu Picchu in 1911. It had been forgotten, lost in the mountain vegetation, since the demise of the Incas in the 16th century.

Although no sculpted or incised stone designs were found, there are some striking sights, especially the Intihuatana or Sundial, the Room of the Three Sisters, the Observatory Tower, and the Royal Tomb and Altar.

Marvels of Paracas

To the south, the people of the Paracas Peninsula, near the port of Pisco, created the world's most beguiling composite iconography of beings with anthropomorphic, zoomorphic and phytomorphic attributes. They were buried in tombs of two different types known as Necropolis (an underground cemetery) and Cavernas (underground cave tombs reached by vertical shafts) in one of the most spellbinding areas on earth, the Paracas Nature Reserve.

The Paracas Peninsula juts out into the Pacific 240 kilometers south of Lima, a marvel of topography that is as dramatic a testimony today to the triumphal apotheosis of nature as it must have been so long ago. Nothing grows on these eroded escarpments and surrounding dunes, blistered as they are by a blazing sun and scourged by the harsh, gritty Paracas wind that gives the area its name. The site's majesty and remoteness are enhanced by spectacular cliff formations—the great arched Catedral or Cathedral, as it is called, and the dramatic obelisk known as the Fraile or Priest.

Islas Ballestas

Offshore, the Islas Ballestas islands provide a dramatic introduction to that ubiquitous resident of the Pacific and South Atlantic coasts of South America, the sea elephant or *lobo del mar*. They can be seen by the hundreds, basking in the sun on rocks beneath the great arches and caves of the jagged hills, while above them wheel sea birds, sources of the guano that, used as fertilizer, fueled the commercial boom of the late 19th century. The sounds here are extraordinary. The strident calls of sea birds, the raucous bellowing of sea elephants and the thundering intermezzos of crashing breakers create a cacophonous ensemble.

This is truly a world where Nature is supreme. Glorious tones of cerulean blue and viridian green water, vivid reds of starfish, flashes of white-breasted penguins and a sulfuric yellow sand of unearthly intensity, all stress the magnificence of this uniquely beautiful place. It is not surprising that reds, yellows and blues constitute such a dominant leitmotiv in much of the virtuoso textile and feather art of the Paracas and Nazca peoples, nor that their art reflects their environment. A magnificent feather work depicting a starfish is a characteristic example.

Pisco: Pisco Sours and a Plaza

Fifteen kilometers along the coast from Paracas is the delightful port of Pisco, as famed for its refreshing grape brew left to ferment in Mediterranean-style amphoras as for a handsome plaza with a statue of San Martín, a fine cathedral and an ornate Municipalidad (Town Hall) dating from 1829.

Nazca Earth Drawings

At Paracas, a huge design of a candelabra etched into the sand of the cliffs points south towards the great Plain of Nazca, 250 kilometers away. The origins of the Candelabra are uncertain; however, there is no doubt about the mysterious "drawings" on the Nazca Plain. Etched about 40 centimeters deep and about one meter wide into the pebble strewn sand, they were created as the testament of the cosmic and religious world-view of a people who

Nazca earth drawing of a whale, estimated to date from between AD 200 and 800. These drawings are scattered across some 200 square kilometers of arid stretches of desert sand and rubble in southern Peru near Nazca, 480 kilometers from Lima. Their figurative and non-figurative art motifs include the human body, spider, monkey, bird and the whale as shown here, as well as geometric shapes.

flourished between about the time of Christ and AD 800. Their figurative themes include birds, a monkey, an impressive whale and many others. As with the geometric motifs, dimensions vary, with some attaining lengths of several kilometers. Perhaps designed for calendrical purposes, they were more probably a tribute offered by mortals to heavenly deities. From these gods came the rays of sunlight and the rain, the latter falling on the mountains and subsequently being transformed into rivers flowing down to make the crops grow on the arid Pacific coast.

Lima's Viceregal Splendors

Lima itself is primarily a colonial and modern city, apart from the unprepossessing ruins of Pachacamac 17 kilometers to the south. It is a large, spread-out metropolis, ringed by ramshackle *barriadas* whose newly rural immigrants have swelled the city's population to between six and seven million people—close to 30 per cent of the nation's total.

Lima's three most interesting *barrios* or neighborhoods are the Centro (Downtown Lima), Bohemian Barranco and fashionable Miraflores, the latter two areas strung out along the high cliffs above the Pacific Ocean. In Lima itself, a good place to start is the city's most imposing square, the Plaza de Armas. Around it are the presidential Palacio de Gobierno, the balconied Archbishop's Palace and the Metropolitan Cathedral. The original 17th-century Cathedral, rebuilt in the mid-18th century, serves as an enlightening introduction to colonial Spanish religious interior art and ornamentation; although many works are clearly European in style, as in the scenes representing the Coronation of the Virgin, others reveal the imprimatur of native Indian artists, who made some of the saints and other figures mestizo. The Cathedral also contains a coffin with the alleged remains of Francisco Pizarro, who was murdered outside it in 1541 and whose nearby equestrian statue is a somber reminder of his ruthless conquest of Peru.

The Inquisition

The sword was sustained by the cloth in colonial South America and the Museo de la Inquisición, a few blocks away, reveals in an often macabre manner that heresy was emphatically not countenanced by the religious authorities. But it's a surprise to discover that in the almost 300 years from 1570 to 1820, notwithstanding Edgar Allan Poe's *The Pit and the Pendulum*, the much maligned and feared Inquisition claimed only about 1,500 victims.

The tradition of Andalusia is very much in evidence in the nearby San Francisco Church, whose decorative interior is reminiscent of Moorish design. Across the adjacent Rimac River the mood is very different in the 16th-century Convento de los Descalzos, a baroque Franciscan monastery. It lies at the end of the Alameda de los Descalzos, the path where La Perricholi, the famous mistress of a Viceroy, used to take her afternoon walks.

In colonial Lima attendance at a major bullfight was a colorful social event, as it is today. The Rimac area's Plaza de Acho is the oldest and most ornate bullring in South America (other countries celebrating the Fiesta Brava include Ecuador, Colombia and Venezuela). Far from being a sport, the *corrida* is a drama with a tragic dimension in which the *torero* must face himself, the crowd and the bull. No wonder that there is always a small chapel in each plaza where *toreros* pray before making the ceremonial *paseo* entry, with their *cuadrilla* teams, into the ring. Dramatic, emotional, and always controversial, the bullfight has probably been best discussed in Ernest Hemingway's classic *Death in the Afternoon* published in the early 1930s.

Plaza San Martín

Lima's second great plaza honors Argentine General José de San Martín, who shares with Simón Bolívar the honor of having liberated South America from Spanish control. Looking onto the Plaza is the traditional Hotel Bolívar, whose charming open terrace is a good place to have an iced Pisco Sour with angostura bitters before looking at some of Lima's outstanding museums.

Lima's Eclectic Museums

The eclecticism of Lima's museums guarantees that those who are not able to get to Cuzco, Machu Picchu, the Paracas Peninsula, the Nazca Earth Drawings/Lines and other salient sites will still have ample opportunity to savor their magic. Each museum has its special attractions. Thus the National Museum of Anthropology and Archaeology, in the Pueblo Libre area, boasts magnificent Paracas textiles, such amazing 2,000-year-old granite carvings as the Chavín Fanged God stela, and huge photographs of the famed Nazca Earth Lines.

Moche Erotic Art

The Americas have very little ancient erotic art. Thus there is a unique significance to the Rafael Larco Herrera Museum's display of numerous ceramics depicting, in explicit and intimate detail, a multiplicity of sexual mores and erotic activities. They are only part of an extraordinary ensemble of some 60,000 ceramic vessels which provide insight into the daily secular and religious life of these pre-Hispanic peoples. The curvilinear stirrup spouts on many of these ceramics were used to pour, at a controlled rate, the *chicha* beverage served to both the living and the dead.

The smaller Museo Amano, also a private museum in the fashionable Miraflores seaside area of Lima, focuses primarily on textiles. Whether woven, embroidered, painted or embellished with feathers or metal, ancient Peruvian weaving, both technically and iconographically, is unequaled in the world. Many of them in fact are harbingers of what would come to be called in the 20th century "modern art"—surely proof of the validity of the concept of the "universal subconscious" whereby people from different times and places nevertheless arrive at similar forms of aesthetic expression.

Andean artists also displayed consummate skill in fashioning gold and silver objects, which vary from delicately wrought representations of peanuts to ferocious large masks, often with turquoise eyes. Some of the greatest works are related to the Lord of Sipán, from the north-coast Moche culture that favored presentation ceremonies involving goblets filled with blood. The most comprehensive display in Lima is in the Museo de Oro, the Gold Museum, whose collection includes an incredible Inca shirt adorned with multiple tiny gold plaques.

Perhaps the best overall generic grouping of all types of pre-Hispanic art is located on the upstairs floor of Lima's stately early 1900s Museo de Arte, situated adjacent to the Italian Museum. It also boasts the finest ensemble of colonial art of the Viceroyalty period—wooden *bargueño* cabinets, religious paintings, furniture, mirrors and characteristic adornments of the years from 1550 to 1820, when Spanish influence was supreme in all of South America. This museum should not be confused with the newer Museo de la Nación, which is located roughly midway between downtown Lima and Miraflores. Its holdings encompass the total scope of Peru's dramatic past, with emphasis on special exhibitions.

Miraflores and the Costa Verde

A welcome break from museum visits could be a trip out to Miraflores, the attractive seaside residential area of Lima. The Cathedral, looking onto the central plaza, is attractive, and from there a 15-minute walk takes one down Avenida Larco to the Malecón, or cliff-side esplanade. This is Lima's famous Costa Verde or Green Coast, a somewhat misleading term as there is relatively little greenery, except for a few palms, cacti and flowers here and there. What it does have are some stunning coastal views, especially from the attractive shopping mall at the end of Larco that has literally been built into the cliff. Below, located on a jetty, is the charming Rosa Nautica Restaurant, its interior and exterior decor echoing the *belle époque* style of early 20th-century Europe. It's a fine place for trying the typical local rice with seafood dish, *arroz con mariscos*, for which Lima is justly famed, while watching surfers coast in on the Pacific waves.

Colonial painting: Coronation of the Virgin with Saints by Miguel de Berrio. After the 16th-century Spanish conquest, artists in South America, including Spanish, indigenous and crillo (the offspring of Spanish and Indian liaisons), produced what is known as "colonial art." Non-Spanish artists could readily adapt to the concept of the Virgin Mary, since for them her pervasive aura was a logical continuation of both the all-powerful Pachamama (Earth Mother) of pre-Hispanic tradition, and of secular, strongly hierarchical Inca government.

Llamas, denizens of the High Andes from Colombia south to Peru, Chile and northwest Argentina.

A woman in the Urubamba Valley area around Cuzco wears the distinctive colorful clothing of the region. This was the site of Inca rule until the arrival of the Spanish conquistadors in 1532.

This 16th-century house in Cuzco is the former home of the Spanish chronicler Garcilaso de la Vega, who was born the son of a Spanish father and an Inca princess.

*The great three-tiered structure of Sacsahuayman lying astride the approaches to Cuzco was built
by the Incas from 200-ton boulders shaped by the simple tools available at the time.*

Alturas de Macchu Pichu was renowned Chilean poet Pablo Neruda's song of praise to the spectacular 8,800-feet high Inca site, lost in Andean mists until discovered by U.S. archaeologist Hiram Bingham in 1911.

The Intihuatana or Sundial at Macchu Pichu.

Exponents of Spanish Viceroyalty architecture, which flourished between 1550 and 1820, built many religious edifices on Inca stone foundations. This Cathedral facing Cuzco's central plaza is one example of such work.

The Candelabra, etched into the sand of a cliffside on the Paracas Peninsula, points to the ancient Nazca earth drawings 250 kilometers to the south.

The Paracas Peninsula, 240 kilometers south of Lima, has 215 varieties of birds, vast colonies of sea elephants and some of the world's most majestic coastal scenery, which includes El Fraile, an imposing natural stone obelisk.

La Catedral, a magnificent arched cliff formation found near the Paracas Peninsula.

Sea elephants bask on the sunlit rocks of Islas Ballestas off Paracas.

*The ornate Municipalidad (Municipality) facing Pisco's main square and located to the
side of the Cathedral was embellished in characteristic early Republican style when constructed in 1829.*

Amphora bottles for storing pisco, a brew made from fermented grapes.

Lima's Cathedral on the stately Plaza de Armas, standing adjacent to the balconied Archbishop's Palace, contains the body of Francisco Pizarro, the conqueror of Peru, who met a violent end in 1541 near the Cathedral doors.

Statue of Francisco Pizarro near Plaza de Armas, Lima. The heroic caudillo or "man on horseback" pose is widely seen in South American statuary.

The charming turn-of-the-century belle époque Rosa Nautica Restaurant, Lima, is situated on a pier jutting out into the Pacific from the suburban Miraflores Costa Verde and offers superb seaside vistas.

Lima's dramatic and precipitous Costa Verde stretches from the suburb of Miraflores, site of an imaginative cliffside development in the 1990s, to historic Barranco in the south.

Feather textile with a starfish design, like the Nazca earth drawings, is a creation of the south coast Peruvian culture that upheld a close affinity with the flora and fauna of the natural world.

In Lima's Plaza de Acho, the most historic bullring in the Americas where toreros like Manolete fought, the Alguacil leads the ceremonial procession that initiates the corrida. Oil sketch by the author (1961).

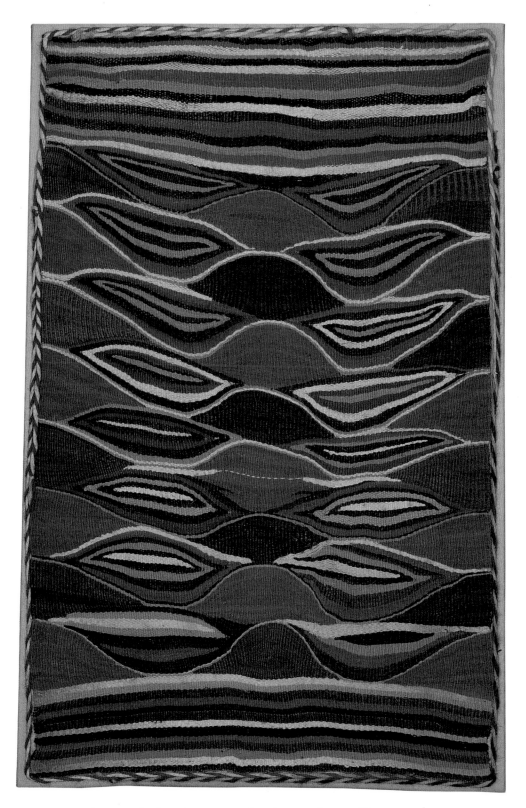

*This example of Nazca tapestry, with an iconography resembling eyes or dunes,
demonstrates the high quality of art to be seen in Lima's museums.*

 Chile, "The Place Where the Land Finishes": A Voyage from Valparaiso to Punta Arenas

Chile, in the ancient Indian Aymara language, means "the place where the land finishes." In Quechua, the language of the ancient Incas still spoken today, *chiri* means cold. Both are possible origins for the name of the country, which is strung out for some 4,630 kilometers from north to south in a long narrow band of terrain whose width varies from about 88 to 368 kilometers. Bounded by the Andes to the east and the Pacific to the west, its 11 million people live in 13 administrative regions. Of these, the most southern is Antarctica, where Chile claims approximately 1.2 million square kilometers.

Chile's island possessions include Juan Fernandez Island, 644 kilometers off the coast, where the shipwreck ordeal of Alexander Selkirk inspired Daniel Defoe's *Robinson Crusoe*, and Easter Island, 3,702 kilometers west of Chile's Pacific coast.

Four Main Topographical Areas

From north to south, Chile has four main topographical areas. The northern part of the country, south from the Peruvian border, to roughly the Copiapo/Coquimbo area, is epitomized by the Atacama desert, repository of minerals and site of the great open pit Chuquicamata Copper mine. The central segment of the country, south to Concepción, has fertile farms and vineyards, as well as the national capital, Santiago, and its great port of Valparaiso. From the Concepción/Temuco area south to Puerto Montt lies the magnificent area of natural splendors with magical names, such as lakes like Llanquihue, waterfalls like Petrohue and volcanoes like Osorno.

South from Puerto Montt, passing the islands of Chiloe and Wellington, and the Taitao Peninsula, one moves towards the majestic world of fjords and inlets, with their snow-capped peaks and mighty glaciers.

Valparaiso

A bustling city of three million people, Valparaiso is a jumble of old and modern buildings in the lower city contrasted with colorful hillside houses that jostle each other and form a pattern like a cubist painting. "Valparaiso, white, pink, gray and green," wrote Salvador Reyes, "ran along the shore and climbed the hills in whimsical designs." Here and there are patches of garden, of new suburbs, of factories, of old houses thrown together at random or balancing on the edge of a ravine. Going up to the top of these hills, either by one of the city's cable cars, by bus or on foot, offers not only splendid views, but can also take you past unusual museums, like the Museo a Cielo Abierto containing murals by Chilean artists.

Two buildings, each striking in its own way, symbolize Chile's past and present. One is the Naval Headquarters building near the port, looking onto a plaza in the centre of which is the Iquique Monument, a memorial of the 1879–83 War of the Pacific and emblem of Chile's reputation for military professionalism. Chile defeated the joint armies of Peru and Bolivia in the war, a theme vividly brought to life in a painting by Encarnación Mirones entitled "A Halt to the Alliance."

A more unprepossessing building is the Legislature, an example of contemporary geometric functionalism that

Simplified Santiago

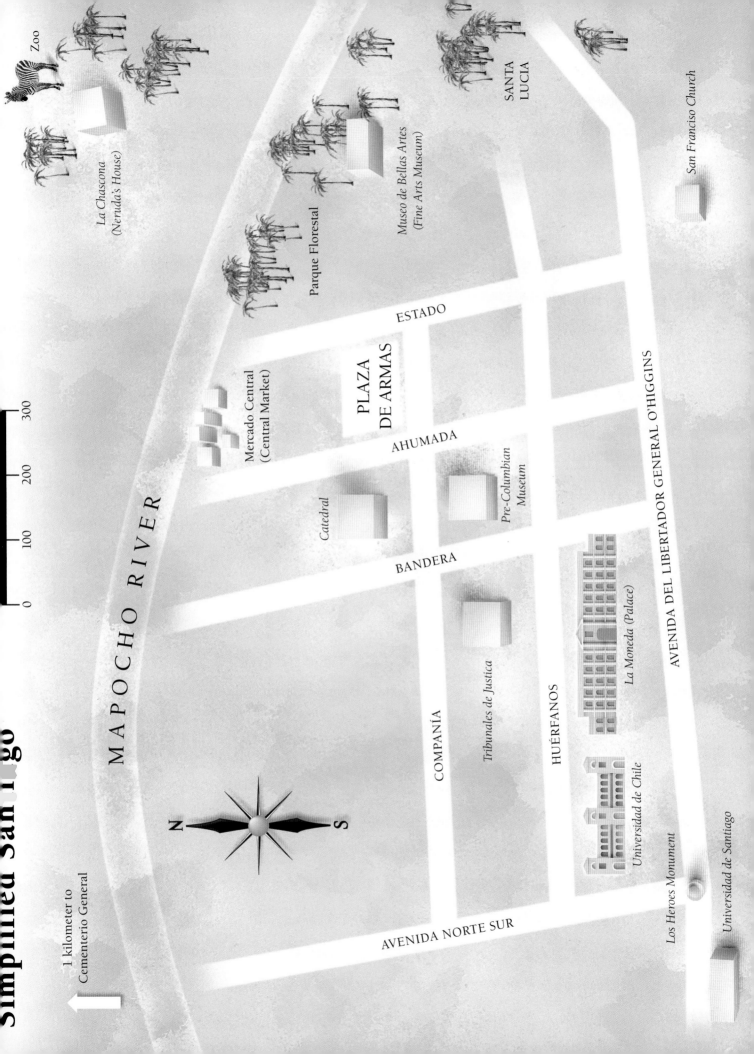

Zoo

La Chascona
(Neruda's House)

1 kilometer to
Cementerio General

MAPOCHO RIVER

300

200

100

0

N

S

SANTA
LUCIA

San Franciso Church

Parque Florestal

Museo de Bellas Artes
(Fine Arts Museum)

ESTADO

Mercado Central
(Central Market)

PLAZA
DE ARMAS

AHUMADA

Catedral

Pre-Columbian
Museum

BANDERA

COMPAÑÍA

Tribunales de Justica

HUÉRFANOS

La Moneda (Palace)

AVENIDA DEL LIBERTADOR GENERAL O'HIGGINS

Universidad de Chile

Los Heroes Monument

Universidad de Santiago

AVENIDA NORTE SUR

was erected during the 16 years from 1973 to 1989 when the Chilean military ran the country. A coup brought the army to power when it overthrew the socialist government of Salvador Allende, the first communist in the world to be elected to office. Its intervention was prompted by the nation's worst ever socio-economic crisis, caused by the stockpiling of arms by Marxist political parties, by leftist efforts to incite rebellion in the armed forces, and by a popular mandate, including that of the Supreme Court, giving power to the military to act.

The government of President Augusto Pinochet, a tough military general, subsequently became involved in a bitter and recriminatory "dirty war" against real or alleged terrorists. It was during this time that Pinochet took the radical step of dividing the government, leaving the Executive and Judiciary in Santiago and establishing the Legislature in Valparaiso.

Viña del Mar

Ranking with Argentina's Mar del Plata and Uruguay's Punta del Este as South America's most elegant seaside resorts, Viña, as it is called, has a beguiling appeal that can best be appreciated in a *paseo* by horse-drawn carriage. Some Tudor-style houses, graceful palm trees in the town's main plaza, a handsome country mansion called the Quinta Vergara and striking seaside vistas are the main attractions. As along the Peruvian Pacific coast, the surf is powerful, the undercurrents strong and the water frequently chilly.

The Quinta Vergara Fine Arts Museum, with paintings evoking 19th-century Chilean life, also has an outdoor theater which hosts a popular annual music festival in February. In the same month there is also a Feria Internacional de Artesanía, with jewelry, art work, leather goods and other products presented in a sophisticated setting.

Pablo Neruda

Along the coast from Valparaiso is Isla Negra, the seaside home of Chile's greatest poet Pablo Neruda (1904–1973). Filled with such eccentric relics as wooden ships' prows carved in the form of women, or an enormous shoe, the house is still pervaded by an atmosphere which reflects the insatiable curiosity and voracious feeling for life that characterizes Neruda's richly fashioned poetry. Its range is eclectic, from the lyrically flowing *Ode to a Nude* to the longer work celebrating the *Heights of Machu Picchu*. Neruda had a house in Valparaiso, La Sebastiana, and one in Santiago (now a museum, it is called La Chascona, a reference to the

Pablo Neruda, Chile's greatest poet and winner of the Nobel Prize for Literature in 1971, was a lifelong defender of humanity against oppression. "There is no space more vast than that of sorrow," he once wrote, "no universe like that which bleeds."

tousled hair of the last lady in his life).

Neruda's dialogue was with the sea, the landscape of his country, strangely shaped "objects at rest", as he called them. But above all it was with his fellow human being, a factor which made him an inveterate foe of dictatorship. One of his poems is illustrative:

La tirania corta la cabeza que canta, pero la voz	Tyranny cuts off the singer's head, but the voice
en el fondo del pozo vuelve a los manantiales	in the depth of the well returns to the earth's
secretos de la tierra y desde la oscuridad	primaeval secrets, and from the darkest depths
sube por la boca del pueblo	soars upwards through the voice of the people.

Santiago

You can get up to Santiago by road from Valparaiso in one to two hours, depending on the traffic. Chile's capital is located in a high valley, with the Andes to the east and coastal mountains to the west. The surrounding mountains, which offer skiing opportunities, create a spectacular setting; however, the city's locale makes it periodically subject to smog. Santiago is not as elegant as Buenos Aires, and not as intimate as Montevideo; but its avenues and parks—especially Cerro Santa Lucía, where Spanish conquistador Pedro Valdivia founded the city in 1541—endow it with a certain charm. The central pedestrian streets, Ahumada and Huérfanos, are some of the nicest places for boutique window-shopping and people-watching in all of South America.

Architects find the city exciting for three reasons: the main railroad station, with its iron framework inspired by the Eiffel Tower in Paris; the late 19th-century Mercado Central or Central Market (pre-fabricated in England), which boasts a Victorian wrought-iron ceiling; and the central cemetery, whose marble mausolea of the élite are rivaled only by those of Punta Arenas in southern Chile, or by the renowned Recoleta cemetery in Buenos Aires.

Plaza de Armas and La Moneda Palace

The city's two major focal points are the Plaza de Armas, graced by the Cathedral and Town Hall, and the Moneda, the name by which the national palace goes since it was originally created as a Mint to make money in 1799. La Moneda was damaged by gunfire in the 1973 coup, and President Allende died there, allegedly taking his own life as he saw his government crumbling.

Museo de Arte Pre-Colombino

For travelers who may not get to Peru or Bolivia, the nearby Museo de Arte Pre-Colombino reveals the extent of the marvelous reality of ancient Andean inventiveness in varied

Pedro Valdivia, the discoverer of Chile and founder of Santiago in 1541. He escaped the fate of his predecessor, Diego de Almagro, whose failure to capture Chile resulted in his execution by Pizarro in 1537. But Valdivia, like many conquistadors, also died violently in the end, allegedly boiled in molten gold by a disgruntled servant.

The huge condor, supreme monarch of the Andes, the rare New World vulture that has a wing span of up to 15 feet, glides speedily down the Peruvian, Chilean and Argentine coast, and can just as easily soar up to the sublime heights of remote snow-capped mountains.

media. The pre-Hispanic textiles, many with figurative and non-figurative iconography that clearly anticipates 20th-century modern art, are another example of the working of the "universal subconscious," which unites people from different continents, climes and chronologies in a similar set of aesthetic criteria.

Puerto Montt: Southern Entry to the Lake District

Some 750 kilometers south of Valparaiso, and 150 kilometers to the north of Chiloe Island, Puerto Montt lies at the north of the Gulf of Ancud. The mighty Andes are just to the east, straddling the border with Argentina that is barely 100 kilometers away; only 75 kilometers further is Argentina's famous mountain resort of San Carlos de Bariloche, with nearby Lake Nahual Huapi and the Llao Llao Hotel.

To the north, for some 320 kilometers as far as Temuco, is Chile's area of picturesquely named volcanoes, lakes and waterfalls, including Llanquihue Lake, Petrohue Waterfall and Osorno Volcano. Puerto Varas, on Lake Llanquihue, has a striking church overlooking the water, some red-roofed houses with rustic rose arbors, snow-capped mountains in the distance and an atmosphere resembling that of parts of Germany or Austria.

Greeting travelers at Puerto Montt's harbor is a fetching llama by the name of Tequila, with the fastidious mannerisms and dainty refinement seen in creatures of the camelid family. Along the port, huge piles of pleasantly fragrant wood chips testify to a dynamic timber industry which, for some observers of the ecological scene, is too dynamic, and may threaten to deplete regional resources. Llamas do not carry humans, but trains do; and there is a brightly painted, fine old model steam locomotive along the Puerto Montt waterfront to remind one of the great railroad days of South America.

The main town of Puerto Montt lies to the right of the harbor dock. A brief kilometer to the left brings one to the lively *feria regional* of San Angelmo. This artisan handicraft market has rather more of an informal and spontaneous feel to it than the one in Viña del Mar, and is enlivened by the peripatetic Tequila and occasional visits of mounted *huaso* Chilean cowboys. Their broad-brimmed hats are colorful items for sale in the market, as are boldly-patterned wool sweaters, ponchos and blankets, as well as articles depicting the ancient mythical figures of Chiloe Island. Nearby is Caleta San Angelmo, the San Angelmo Cove with fishing boats of kaleidoscopic hues and a good view across a short stretch of water to Tenglo Island.

The Realm of the Condor: South from Puerto Montt

To the south of Puerto Montt, one begins the great odyssey into the realm of the condor, the monarch of the Andes who soars with his immense wing span over a secluded and infinite world. This is a special universe, a place to commune with nature and with the Absolute, a place where humans seem lost in the immensity of untrammeled splendor and of implacable solitude.

"Drowning in the Wind"

Solitude . . . Chile is a land of brilliant literary figures, not only of the famed Nobel Prize winners Pablo Neruda and Gabriela Mistral, but of others like Oscar Castro and Manuel Rojas, who are sensitive to the magic of their land and to the solitude which it induces. Metaphors abound to describe this state, particularly in relation to the mountains, fjords and glaciers. "The solitude of high altitudes," writes Oscar Castro, "is so wide, so diaphanously unsheltered, that at times the traveler feels the airy sensation of drowning in the wind." For Manuel Rojas, it can be almost apocalyptic: "Solitude seems to dominate everything; it is overwhelming; a solitude which seems to throb in the darkness or in the moonlight, a solitude which waylays you and joins you, surrounds you, threatens you, isolates you and also defends you; nobody will look for you in that solitude. . ."

This overwhelming solitude is the essence of the marvelous reality of southern Chile, particularly for those who can appreciate its pristine beauty, as Magellan, Cook and Darwin once did, from the deck of a ship. Here indeed exists the opportunity for contemplation, introspection and for meditation that all too often eludes us. But down here, in these remote southern climes, the light can be ephemeral, with the weather changing suddenly from bleakly sullen skies to vistas of sunlit brilliance, from pale gray clouds to a roseate Arcadian afterglow in the crepuscular light of evening.

As for the mood, it can be austere, as when veils of nebulous mist swirl upwards past somber glaciers flanked by cold black rocks to envelop snow-capped peaks. But when the sun shines, the huge fissures of ice in the five-kilometer wide Pius XI Glacier undergo a lyrical metamorphosis, a transformation into thousands of towering cathedral spires glistening in pale blue, white and gold. It is in such an otherworldly place that the sublime transcendence of nature casts us into deep reverie. It reveals to us, in Mariano Latorre's words, how "The untrodden snow of the glaciers and snowdrifts whitens the ground and covers the bare hills. Its own frozen heart melts lower down in foaming skeins, in white arms of water."

Few mortals would venture into these beautiful but forbidding climes. But in the mid-19th century, defying the odds, a remarkable community developed on the western banks of the Strait of Magellan. Its sandy banks attracted attention, and so it came to be called Punta Arenas, or Sandy Point.

Punta Arenas: Early Development

Punta Arenas, Chile's most southern port, is one of the least known, yet most fascinating small towns of South America. It embodies romance and entrepreneurial bravado and serves as an exemplary display of how well the "melting pot" theory could work in the New World.

Capital of Magallanes Region and 2,300 kilometers south of Valparaiso, Punta Arenas was founded as a military garrison and penal settlement in 1848. Five years earlier, in 1843, Chilean President Bulnes had established Chile's first outpost in the Magallanes Region at the fort that bears his name. The route to Fort Bulnes, 60 kilometers due south from Punta Arenas, takes one past native hardwood forests of *coigue* and *lenga*, and past Tonina dolphins cavorting along the shores of the Straits of Magellan.

Important Commercial Location

Punta Arenas became an important port for ships rounding southern South America en route to California during the mid-19th-century gold rush. Rather than going around Cape Horn, ships in the Atlantic Ocean could reach the Pacific via the Strait of Magellan or the Beagle Channel.

To reach Punta Arenas from the Atlantic there are two routes. A ship either sails southwest through the Strait of Magellan, or approaches the port via the Beagle Channel further to the south, turning west into the Channel in the vicinity of the three islands of Picton, Nueva and Lennox. It would be over those three bleak, inhospitable and rocky outcrops that Argentina and Chile were ready to fight a war in 1979! A conflict, in fact, was only avoided by the timely intervention of the papal emissary Cardinal Samore, whose bust stands on Calle Colón near the turn-of-the-century Chilean Air Force Club. It is located just before the large mosaic mural on Calle O'Higgins honoring Chilean Nobel Prize-winning poet Gabriela Mistral.

Once in the Beagle Channel, ships proceeded to the west, then turned north into the Straits of Magellan for the short distance to Punta Arenas, on the western side of the straits.

The Golden Age of Punta Arenas

In the second half of the 19th century, commercial and agricultural expansion brought European immigrants, and a dynamic entrepreneurial spirit. Prosperity was fueled by timber, seal-hunting, gold, import and export commerce, coal, and sheep farming. In 1895 the first telephone was installed, and by 1900 Punta Arenas was at its apogee.

The only woman in South America to win the Nobel Prize for Literature, Gabriela Mistral was as sensitive to humanity as to the beauty of her country's landscape. "By the end of May," she observed, "the countryside, overtaken by winter, loses its golden-green abundance of grains and fruits."

El Ovejero—The Sheepherder as Symbol

Along Avenida Bulnes near the city's famed cemetery is a handsome bronze monument to a sheepherder, his dog, horse and sheep. Beside it there is a plaque with a poignant inscription by José Granada:

El Ovejero de mi Tierra	The Sheepherder of my Land
Es un símbolo Viviente	Is a living symbol
del empuje y la paciencia	of courage and patience
frente al viento que lo curte	scourged by cutting winds
y al silencio que lo aprieta	and by oppressive silence.

The statue is a vivid reminder that mutton, wools and skins were the driving economic force of Punta Arenas in the late 19th century. Within a few decades of the importation of 300 pure-bred sheep from the Falkland Islands, sheep in the local Magallanes Region had proliferated to the astonishing figure of more than two million!

The thrust behind this dynamic economic growth was the influx of a widely varying spectrum of European settlers. Immigrants came from Switzerland, England, Wales and Croatia. The most powerful families, however, originated in Russia and the Baltic, Portugal, Spain and France, notably the Russians Elias and Sofía Hamburger de Braun, from Talsen in the Kurland Russian Baltic area; the Spaniards José Menendez and José Montes; the Portuguese José Nogueira and the Frenchman Juan Blanchard.

The evidence of their prestige and influence is apparent from the architecture in and around Punta Arenas' central Plaza Muñoz Gamero. The plaza itself, a congenial forum of social life, has a bust of José Menendez and a bandstand kiosk beneath the trees. Its focal point is a magnificent statue of Magellan above a grouping of local Indians representing Patagonia and Tierra del Fuego. Dutifully touching the foot of one of them is recommended, as it is said to bring good luck.

Chile's Indians like the Tehuelche, Alacufe and Mapuche never had much luck in dealing with either the Spaniards or the subsequent European immigrants. There are still several hundred thousand Mapuche Indians living up around the Temuco area, the heirs of those who fought the Spaniards in a 300-year war. The Spaniards called the Mapuches Araucanians, after Alonso de Ercilla y Cuñiga penned his famous poem *La Araucana* in 1560.

Stately Mansions

Indications are that the local indigenous population of the Punta Arenas region fared no better at the hands of 19th-century immigrants than they had under the Spaniards. Certainly the frontier spirit, the tough challenges and the ambition of the local captains of industry were not factors conducive to protection of their rights.

The mansions in the vicinity of Plaza Muñoz Gamero reflect the power and prestige of the great families that had established themselves by 1900. Many of them were linked by marriage and commercial enterprises, and tracing their family trees is a fascinating study in the evolution of turn-of-the-century southern Chilean society and wealth.

A good place to start, next to the Army Officers Club, is the ornate residence of José Menendez. Across the Plaza on the corner of Calle Magallanes, you can see the successful commercial establishment which he ran with his wife Maria Behety. There were seven children from this marriage and one of them, Josefina, married Mauricio Braun. Their mansion, now the Magallanes Regional Historical Museum, is located half a block from Plaza Muñoz Gamero and was built in 1904 by the French architect André Beaulieu. Wandering through its well-appointed rooms, replete with billiard table, elegant furniture, statuary, mementos and period photographs, one gains a remarkable insight into what society life one hundred years ago was like in Punta Arenas.

Mauricio Braun's sister, Sara Braun, was by all accounts a remarkable women. She was married to an older man, the Portuguese José Nogueira after whom the hotel at the corner of the Plaza is named, but was widowed at an early age. Her individualism, sometimes viewed in a controversial light in terms of her human relationships, is well represented in the magnificent "palace" which she had built in 1895 at the corner of the Plaza adjacent to the Nogueira Hotel. Its neoclassical facade and interior evoke the *belle époque* era from 1850 to 1914, while the embellished ceilings suggest an 18th-century decorative rococo style. Later preserved by the Magallanes Club de la Unión, the building was declared a historical monument in 1982.

Other impressive eye-catching residences on the Plaza Muñoz Gamero are those of José Montes (now the Town Hall), and Juan Blanchard (now the Banco Edwards). And, nearby, there is an ornate building that was traditionally the Firefighters Center.

The second place that depicts the wealth of Punta Arenas during its golden age is the palatial cemetery, with spectacular and, in the eyes of some people, ostentatious structures, like that of José Menendez. His Italianate mausoleum is considered to imitate in style and design that of King Victor Emanuel of Italy. Notable also are the many Croatian names on tombstones testifying to one of the largest Croatian colonies in the New World.

Conclusion

In considering Punta Arenas' dramatic development after 1850, it is often forgotten that no settlement was established there in the preceding 330 years that had elapsed since the strait on which it is located was discovered. The discovery of that strait, and indeed of the adjacent areas of Patagonia and Tierra del Fuego, is one of the epic adventures of the age of discovery. The story of that dramatic discovery by Ferdinand Magellan assumes a special meaning for those who sail through these fabled waters.

Houses scattered in haphazard fashion over Valparaiso hillsides form a cubist composition in the old section of Chile's largest port.

The geometric facade of the Chilean Parliament building reflects General Pinochet's decision, when he was President, to divide the legislature in Valparaiso from the executive and judiciary branches of government in Santiago.

The elegant Quinta Vergara Museum epitomizes the atmosphere of Viña del Mar, Chile's chic, perennially fashionable and international seaside resort adjacent to Valparaiso.

The Iquique Monument in front of Valparaiso Naval Headquarters, seen in the background, recalls Chile's celebrated victory over Peru and Bolivia in the 1879–1883 War of the Pacific.

Detail of a striking painting, "Alto a la Alianza" ("Halting the Alliance"), by popular 19th-century artist Encarnación Mirones, which recreates Chile's epic triumphs in the War of the Pacific.

With a lofty elevation flanked by two mountain chains, Santiago, the capital of Chile,
offers magnificent panoramic views of snow-capped peaks.

Ancient Andean textiles are among the treasured collections at the Museo de Arte Pre-Colombino in Santiago. This striking example of painted textile was created almost 1,000 years ago.

Stately Santiago is a city that combines modern architecture with spacious plazas and avenues.

La Moneda, the presidential palace and seat of power in Santiago, was the scene of dramatic events during the 1973 military golpe de estado resulting in the overthrow and death of communist President Salvador Allende.

Plaque to Tupahue in the Sacred Place of God on Cerro Santa Luciá, atop the wooded hill where Spanish conquistador Pedro de Valdivia officially founded Santiago in the 16th century.

(Above) With woodchips destined for export in the background, Puerto Montt llama, Tequila, greets arriving visitors.

(Left) The artisans' market of Puerto Montt in adjacent San Angelmo displays the region's colorful arts and crafts.

Ancient steam locomotive along the Puerto Montt waterfront evokes the heyday of railroad travel.

Puerto Montt is the gateway to such famed lakes as nearby Llanquihue, seen here with Mount Osorno rising serenely above its placid waters.

A glimpse of the awesome San Rafael glacier in southern Chile.

The magnificent Pope Pius XI Glacier, one of the world's most spectacular, extends across a width of five kilometers.

(Left) Opulent mausolea, like that of José Menendez, scion of one of Punta Arenas' great families, testify to the southern Chilean port's great prosperity in the early 1900s, when Balkan, Portuguese and northern European settlers arrived.

(Right) Boldly rendered modern bronze sculpture on Avenida Bulnes.

Handsome bronze sculpture on Avenida Bulnes of a shepherd with his horse, dog and flock of sheep is a vivid reminder that mutton, wool and skins were Punta Arenas' driving economic force in the "golden age" between 1890 and 1914.

(Right) Schoolchildren pose beneath a bust of José Menendez in Plaza Muñoz Gamero, central Punta Arenas.

(Below) A shaded bandstand kiosk in Plaza Muñoz Gamero; behind is the Town Hall, once the mansion of José Montes.

(Above)This neoclassical 1895 house was once the home of Sara Braun, widow of Portuguese entrepreneur José Nogueira in whose honor the adjoining hotel is named. The house is now a historical monument preserved by the Magallanes Club de la Unión.

(Left) Interior of the Sara Braun house.

In the José Nogueira Hotel, the charming Pérgola Restaurant provides a comfortable setting to sample Chile's excellent red and white wines.

Photograph of 19th-century military personages are reminders that Punta Arenas was founded in 1848 as a garrison and penal settlement.

The Magallanes Regional Historical Museum, once the very well appointed residence of Mauricio Braun and Josefina Menendez, was built in 1895 by French architect André Beaulieu.

Inside the former Braun-Menendez residence, the billiard room, refined statuary, sophisticated furnishings, family mementos and period photographs provide an intriguing insight into society life in Punta Arenas at the turn of the century.

LA   MUNICIPALIDAD   DE   PUNTA   ARENAS

A

GABRIELA MISTRAL

1991

This huge tile mosaic pays tribute to Chile's most famous female poet, Nobel Prize winner Gabriela Mistral.

Three remarkable men belong irrevocably to the seafaring pantheon of southern South America—the Portuguese Ferdinand Magellan, and the Englishmen Captain James Cook and Charles Darwin. Cook's visit was brief, but those of the others were more extensive and of far-reaching consequence.

Epic Voyage

On September 20, 1519, the Portuguese Fernão de Magalhaes, better known by his Spanish name Ferdinand Magellan, set sail under the auspices of Holy Roman Emperor Charles V—also King of Spain Charles I—on a momentous undertaking. His goal was to reach the Spice Isles and fabled wealth of Cathay by finding a sheltered passage and navigable route round southern South America that would take him from the Atlantic to the Pacific

Ocean. What would turn out to be a voyage around the world would end three years later, in September 1522; Magellan, by then, would be dead, and of the original expedition of 237 men and five ships—*Trinidad, Concepción, San Antonio, Santiago* and *Victoria*—only the *Victoria*, with 18 survivors, would limp back to Spain.

An incredible feat! But these were years of supreme individualism, of men acting alone to impose their will on both the known and the unknown. Appalling living conditions, brutally inclement weather, animosity from his Spanish captains, mutinies by his crew, terrible moments of doubting himself—all failed to blunt his resolve. Magellan himself would die in a tragic incident with natives at Mactan, in the Philippines, in December 1521; but by then he had made his mark. He had sailed across the Atlantic, down the east coast of South America, and harbored at Port St Julian in Argentina, amid the still infernal winds of Necochea and Bahía Blanca. Then he had pushed further

It was Ferdinand Magellan's unflagging resolve and courageous leadership that helped him overcome obstacles and led to his discovery of the South American strait that bears his name.

Magellan and Darwin Exploration

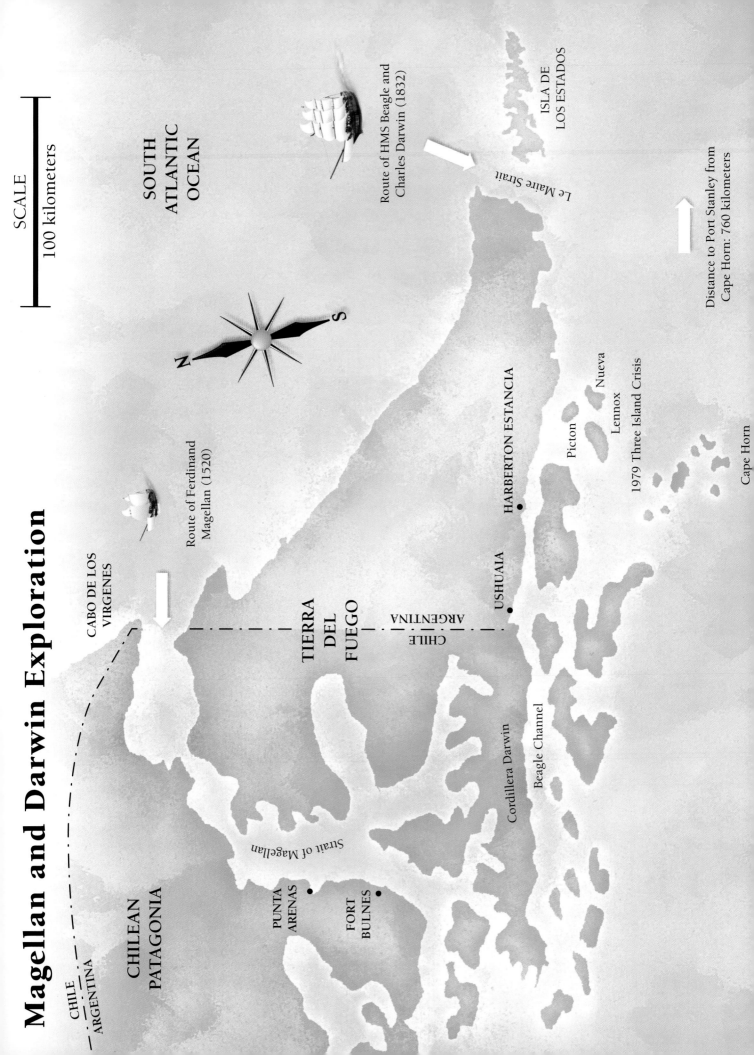

CHILE
ARGENTINA

SCALE
100 kilometers

SOUTH
ATLANTIC
OCEAN

Route of HMS Beagle and
Charles Darwin (1832)

ISLA DE
LOS ESTADOS

Le Maire Strait

Distance to Port Stanley from
Cape Horn: 760 kilometers

N S

Route of Ferdinand
Magellan (1520)

HARBERTON ESTANCIA

Picton

Nueva

Lennox

1979 Three Island Crisis

Cape Horn

CABO DE LOS
VIRGENES

USHUAIA

TIERRA
DEL
FUEGO

ARGENTINA

CHILE

CHILEAN
PATAGONIA

Cordillera Darwin

Beagle Channel

Strait of Magellan

PUNTA
ARENAS

FORT
BULNES

south, finally turning inland to the west at Cabo de los Vírgenes—the Cape of the Virgins—the eastern extremity of what became known as the Strait of Magellan.

Here he sent the *San Antonio* and *Concepción* on ahead to reconnoiter, only to think that they had been lost in a savage storm. Their unexpected return, with news that tests of saltwater flows and equally balanced flood and ebb tides indicated an open passage to the ocean to the west, was a rare occasion for rejoicing.

The Strait of Magellan was not simple to navigate. On the contrary, its inhospitable environment, complex topography and challenging maritime conditions taxed Magellan's ingenuity to the full. The word "strait" in fact is highly misleading; it is in reality a waterway made up of a maze of inlets, bays, fjords and alternating forks where volatile weather, strong currents, narrow passages, brusque *williwaw* winds, rocky outcrops and sudden shallow areas are formidable challenges even for the most consummate navigator.

Looking for the "Wonders of the World"

What we know about Magellan's odyssey is largely due to the chronicle of Antonio Pigafetta, an Italian who went along with Magellan to see at first hand the "Wonders of the World." He gives a vivid account, not only of the discovery of the Strait of Magellan, but also of the origin of the words "Patagonia" and "Tierra del Fuego." Patagonia covers the vast area of land stretching some 1,500 kilometers south from the area of Bahía Blanca to Río Gallegos, and ending close to where Tierra del Fuego begins. "Patagao," or "big-foot," Pigafetta says, was the name given by the Spaniards to a certain South American Indian who was so tall, "that we reached only to his waist belt."

Shakespeare, *The Tempest* and Setebos

The Indians' naive friendliness, however, was their downfall. Since Magellan had been given orders from the Casa de la Contratación to collect and take back to Spain new human varieties encountered on his expeditions, the Spaniards treacherously tricked the ingenuous Patagaos into putting irons on their legs. Taken aboard Magellan's ships, the hapless Indians rapidly died. Their desperate invocations to their god Setebos would be borrowed by William Shakespeare for use by Caliban in the play *The Tempest*.

As for Tierra del Fuego, the large island at the southern tip of Argentina whose northern shore is separated from

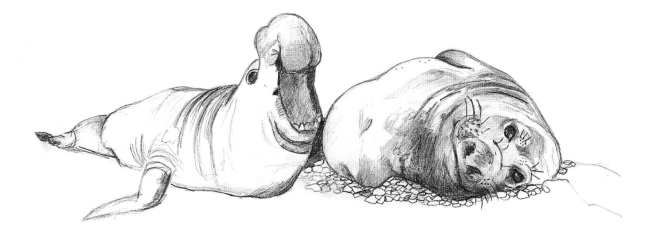

From the south of Peru and around to Argentina, the huge sea elephant
is one of South America's most impressive denizens, living as they do in huge colonies in such imposing domains as the
great arched cliffs of the Islas Ballestas, near the Paracas Peninsula. Few things can equal the cacophony created by the
raucous bellowing of these gargantuan creatures at mating time.

Patagonia by the Strait of Magellan, it was called "Land of Fire" because the Spaniards saw flickering flames along the shore caused by the constant burning of dry grass and wood by the local Indians.

Captain Cook and HMS *Endeavour*

Some 250 years later, a man whose seafaring exploits would rival those of Magellan, and whose life would also end violently on a remote Pacific island, also reached Tierra del Fuego. The Englishman Captain James Cook had sailed from Plymouth aboard HMS *Endeavour* on August 26, 1768, on an Admiralty mission to observe the transit of Venus near Tahiti. He was accompanied by two remarkable men, the botanists Joseph Banks and Daniel Solander. Their route took them across the Atlantic, down the east coast of South America via Rió de Janeiro, and thence to Tierra del Fuego. But the stop in January 1769, marred by the loss of two men in a snowstorm during a scientific foray led by Banks, was brief; the *Endeavour* then proceeded south, and was fortunate to have a relatively tranquil passage around the Cape.

Darwin and the *Voyage of the Beagle*

A little over 60 years after Cook's visit, another remarkable figure in the lore of southern South America would sail both along the northern and southern shores of Tierra del Fuego. In December 1832, the British naturalist Charles Darwin would explore its southern shore, through the Beagle Channel, and in January and May 1834 he would be in the eastern reaches of the Strait of Magellan. Prior to this, however, Darwin had visited the windswept islands 600 kilometers to the east of Cape Horn that the British know as Falklands and the Argentine call Las Malvinas. In the intervening years since Darwin's visit, these remote islands would undergo some dramatic moments, especially in 1914 and in 1982.

Charles Darwin and HMS *Beagle* in the Falkland Islands

Charles Robert Darwin, whose father was a famed physician and naturalist, set out at the age of 22 on December 27, 1831 to serve as the unpaid naturalist on a survey ship, the ten-gun brig HMS *Beagle* under Royal Naval Captain Fitzroy. His Botany professor at Cambridge, John Henslow, had secured him the chance, and during the almost five years that the voyage lasted young Darwin benefited from it to the maximum. His observations on topography, flora and fauna would serve as the basis for his revolutionary 1859 theory of natural selection expounded in *On the Origin of Species by Means of Natural Selection*.

The *Beagle*'s course from England and into the South Atlantic would take her to the islands which the British call Falklands, and which the Argentines refer to as Malvinas. Darwin summed them up as consisting of "an undulating land with a wretched and desolate aspect, peaty soil and wiry grass." This does not do the area justice. The hundreds of islands, of which East and West Falkland are the most important, are spread across an area 256 kilometers wide. They contain magnificent coastlines, rolling moorlands and grassy plains, white quartz sand beaches, dramatic cliffs fringed by coils of huge kelp, fragrant cinnamon grass, a surprisingly temperate climate and an exhilaratingly pure air and light which enhance nature's splendors to the full.

Falklands Flora and Fauna

There is also a lively ensemble of fauna, varying from approximately 570,000 sheep to southern sea lions, sea elephants and fur seals and an eclectic selection of birds and penguins. The latter include the Magallanic Jackass, Gentoo, Rockhopper, Macaroni and King varieties. Among examples of other fauna, there are the black-brown albatross and the thin-billed prion. And, above all, this has always been the haunt of whales, whose tragic past is

Of the many different species of penguins in southern South America and Antarctica Charles Darwin was especially taken by the Falklands Jackass variety. It is so called, he narrates, "from its habit, while on shore, of throwing its head backwards and making a large strange noise, very like the braying of an ass."

recalled in a telling image at Port Stanley. It is a mounted harpoon gun and, next to it, a poignant message: "20,000 whales were killed by this gun between 1937 and 1965."

Kelpers

The 2,200 residents, just over 1,200 of whom live in the capital Port Stanley, are known as "Kelpers"—a name derived from the kelp which Darwin describes as *macrocystis pyrifera*, growing on every rock "from low water mark to a great depth" with a "round, slimy and smooth stem" and attaining depths of several hundred feet. They are subjects of the Falkland Islands, a Dependent Territory of the United Kingdom where the Queen's authority is exercised by a Governor advised by a local elected Executive Council. The Kelpers' existence is a truly remote one. They are 12,800 kilometers (8,500 miles) south of the United Kingdom, 560 kilometers (350 miles) east of the Argentine coast and 1,600 kilometers (1,000 miles) north of Antartica.

History of Political Turmoil

Darwin was in the area at a time of political turmoil that is reflected, even today, in the conflicting claims of Argentina and Britain to ownership of the islands. The Argentines argue that five points validate their *de jure* right to the Islas Malvina. First, that Pope Alexander's 1494 Tordesillas Treaty line and the 1506 Papal Bull placed the area within Spanish jurisdiction. The discovery of the islands by one of Magellan's captains, Esteban Gomez, likewise placed them under Spanish rule. They thus logically became Argentine when Argentina achieved its independence from Spain in the early 19th century; Argentine occupation of the islands between 1826 and 1833 further corroborated their sovereignty, which was brusquely truncated by British seizure. Finally, the Argentines argue, the geographical proximity of the Islas Malvinas to Argentina make Argentine sovereignty logical.

The British claim is essentially a *de facto* one, based upon the discoveries of early mariners. The first reported sighting was reportedly that of Elizabethan navigator John Davis and his ship *Desire*. This was followed by Sir John Hawkins' appearance in the outlying Jason Islands in 1594, and then by the arrival of Captain John Strong, whose sloop *Welfare* made the first landing on the islands in 1690.

Britain asserts that the Spanish were never interested in the South Atlantic area, abandoning it after they had lost 3,500 settlers in the Strait of Magellan area by 1588. Furthermore, the British aver, England occupied the island from 1766 to 1774, at a time when the Spanish renunciation of claims in 1771 enabled the British to establish their sovereignty. Although the British admit that they too abandoned the area in 1774, they left behind a metal plaque which, according to international law, testified to British sovereignty.

London's most cogent arguments, however, are modern-day ones: that "self-determination" is a leitmotiv of United Nations philosophy, and the decision of the Kelpers is uncompromisingly to remain under the aegis of the United Kingdom. The final argument is a pragmatic one, based on the *uti possidetis* doctrine: the British have owned the islands for 150 years, and readjustment of frontiers is now neither realistic nor practical.

This maelstrom of political bickering seems to have been forgotten to the visitor to Port Stanley. As one wanders past Victorian-style houses with gardens aglow with lupins and hollyhocks, the atmosphere is strongly British. Christ Church Cathedral rises over the waterfront as an affirmation of the Protestant faith. The adjacent Ross Square is adorned with the lower jawbones of two sperm whales installed in 1933 to mark the island's centenary under British control. Just beyond is a vestige of the 19th century: the Upland Goose Hotel, formerly called the Eagle Inn and Ship Hotel and also the birthplace in 1871 of the lovely Ellaline Terriss, who went to England to become an actress and the toast of the Edwardian era.

A little further on Ross Road brings one to something of an architectural anomaly—the New School. Set several hundred meters back from the waterfront, this is an impressive 1992 construction whose eminently functional geometric architecture looks somewhat incongruous. It was financed by revenues from the Islands' most lucrative source of income—licensing fees from the 150-mile Fishery Zone. Nearby is the more reassuringly traditional Governor's Residence and the local Museum.

The latter, ironically the former house of the local Argentine director of the LADE air service that linked Argentina and the Falklands before the 1982 war, is well worth a visit. The dedicated curator John Smith, an import from England, is an enthusiastic guide to the Museum's diverse memorabilia of local life. These include a magnificent 19th-century symphonion, badly damaged during the 1982 fighting in Port Stanley and subsequently restored to its former state thanks to John Smith's astute judgment and canny skills. Of special interest are photographs and mementos related to British Admiral John Sturdee, whose naval triumph against Germany in the Port Stanley area in 1914 insured British naval supremacy in the South Atlantic for the duration of the First World War until the Armistice in November 1918.

The Great Naval Battle of December 8, 1914

Along Ross Road, an imposing memorial with classical figures surmounted by an Elizabethan ship pays tribute to this British naval triumph. On the morning of December 8, 1914, an observer of the Falkland Islands Defense Force was astonished to see the German Pacific Fleet, consisting of the *Dresden, Gneisenau, Scharnhorst, Nurnberg* and *Leipzig*, approaching the Islands! Fortuitously, Admiral Sturdee's squadron of two battle cruisers, the *Invincible* and *Inflexible*, and five cruisers—the *Kent, Cromwell, Bristol, Glasgow* and *Carnarvon*—was ready for the confrontation, the latter three cruisers still smarting from an earlier defeat by the Germans at the battle of Coronel off the Chilean coast a few days before.

The ships opened fire at ranges of between eight and 12 kilometers, with disastrous results for the Kaiser's navy. During the day, four German ships were sunk, with only the *Dresden* slipping away to gain a temporary respite until she too went down. The British lost no ships. The total loss of life on that one December day, close to 2,500, was more than twice that sustained in the two-and-a-half-month war between Britain and Argentina in March 1982.

1982 and the War That Never Should Have Happened

The 1982 conflict between Britain and Argentina is also commemorated in another Ross Road monument. But this one is austere in its stark simplicity. Large letters on the simple stone memorial offer a simple but profound tribute: "TO THOSE WHO LIBERATED US IN 1982."

Why did the 1982 war occur between Argentina and Britain, a country which played a major role in Argentine socio-economic development in the 19th century, and whose descendants today comprise a colony of 100,000 Anglo-Argentines in Buenos Aires? The answer lies largely in the chronological context—the year 1982.

This was a time when the Argentine military government was becoming increasingly unpopular after being in power since its summary removal of Isabela Perón from the presidency in the mid-1970s. Generals Videla, Viola and Galtieri, who had followed each other in succession, had been preoccupied with an unpleasant anti-terrorist struggle that came to be known as *La Guerra Sucia*, the "Dirty War." It had sinister and unsavory ramifications: a suspected 10–15,000 *desaparecidos*, real or imagined opponents of the regime, "disappeared," as it was euphemistically put, although they had in all probability been killed.

The country was also beset by other critical problems. National economic output was falling, wages were decreasing, unemployment and inflation were increasing vertiginously and, in early 1982, there were alarming signs of popular unrest in such Buenos Aires working-class suburbs as Avellaneda.

It is an old adage that nothing unifies a country in trouble better than the real or perceived threat of an enemy. For a ruling Argentine military junta of army, navy and air force commanders with their backs to the ropes, there was no better enemy than Britain, flaunting her colonialism in the South Atlantic by exerting sovereignty over territory to which they believed Argentina had a historic right! And this was not only the rationale of military men desperate to galvanize the public into a show of unity. The strongly nationalist Foreign Minister Costa Mendes was also an ardent proponent of Argentina's rights to sovereignty over the Malvinas.

Sovereignty: the Key Issue

There might have been compromises reached over the issue of sovereignty, such as a joint Argentine/British condominium sharing arrangement, or a leaseback agreement, whereby Argentina would have sovereignty over the Islands and would lease all or part of them to Britain. But it seems unlikely that the Kelpers, witnessing events in Argentina in the 1970s and early 1980s, would have acquiesced in such solutions. It is also improbable that London would have adopted such measures against the express wishes of the Kelpers.

Fantastic Reality

Part of the marvelous reality of South America is the aura of fantasy that periodically envelops its secular and religious institutions. General Galtieri, with his pistol holsters emulating those of General Patton, is in a sense as fantastic a figure as O Conselheiro, the Brazilian religious fanatic who took on the Brazilian Army in the late 19th century, and who is the subject of Mario Vargas Llosa's remarkable literary work *The War of the End of the World*. Galtieri was a product of the myth of the invincibility of the Argentine soldier-leader, around whom hung the air of past military triumphs, and whose person, embellished by glittering uniforms, would be shown to the crowds in spectacular four-hour annual parades through the elegant sectors of Buenos Aires, with radio and television announcers recalling grandiose military accomplishments and traditions.

And so the military junta implemented "Operation Blue"—originally titled "Operation Rosary" to suggest the idea of a semi-religious crusade. It involved dispatching a landing force, Task Force 40 comprising just over 900 men, to seize Port Stanley on April 2, 1982 from a defensive force of less than 100 British marines. The successful operation immediately enhanced Galtieri's popularity. The country was momentarily electrified with pride, popular enthusiasm exploding like that of the euphoric shouts of *hinchas*—fans—cheering at a soccer match. All this was short-lived. The conscript troops, it turned out, were not only ill-equipped for the rugged Falkland terrain and climate; worse still, the men in power had made a monumental miscalculation about the British response.

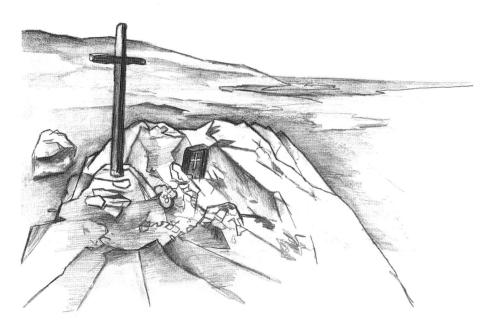

*An austere monument on Mount Tumbledown,
over a strategic approach to Port Stanley, honors the five Scots Guards killed
and more than 30 wounded in the final British assault
by General Jeremy Moore's forces,
which secured the capital and ended the 1982 war on June 14.*

Perhaps the junta commanders should have recalled Lord Nelson's exhortation at Trafalgar: "England expects every man to do his duty." If they were right in knowing that Britain had lost her colonial empire, they were totally wrong in assuming she had lost her pride and will. There was another significant factor which they failed to take into consideration: Prime Minister Margaret Thatcher. She was languishing in the political doldrums at the time, and she recognized in the arrogant Argentine seizure of the Falklands a heaven-sent opportunity to retrieve her reputation. She would retake the Falklands and thereby rally the British people behind her. The result was a 70-ship armada that sailed from England on a recovery mission that ended with British forces under Major General Jeremy Moore recapturing Port Stanley on 14 June.

The performance of the Argentine army and navy forces during the war merits little mention. The air force, however, using sophisticated Exocet missiles, acquitted itself with distinction, as the British ships *Sheffield*, *Atlantic Conveyor*, *Ardent*, *Antelope* and *Sir Galahad* found to their cost. The most serious casualties occurred when the British submarine HMS *Conqueror* sank the 13,600-ton cruiser *General Belgrano*, with a loss of life of 321 navy personnel and two civilians. At the end of the war, total Argentine casualties were just under 650, while those of the United Kingdom were 255.

The biggest casualty of the war, however, was the downfall of General Galtieri as President, and the demise—probably irrevocable—of *de facto* military governmental rule.

The Aftermath

Foreign visitors to the Falkland Islands today are surprised at the bitterness with which many Kelpers continue to view Argentina. This is regrettable, because the attitudes of the Argentine civilian governments since 1982 have had nothing to do with dictatorial militarism. Rather, the *démarches* made during the 1990s by Argentina's distinguished Foreign Minister, Guido di Tella, in the government of President Saul Meném, have been enlightened, positive and sophisticated. Aimed as much at rapprochement with Britain as with the Falklands' Kelpers, they reflect the civilized rationale which has characterized much of Argentina's conduct in the past. Perhaps a new generation will view neighboring Argentina in a different light, and work out an accommodation which will bring many of Argentina's assets to the Islands.

Le Maire Strait and Nueva, Picton and Lennox Islands

Having finished with Patagonia and the Falkland Islands, Darwin goes on to describe his "first arrival in Tierra del Fuego. A little after noon we doubled Cape St Diego, and entered the famous Strait of Le Maire." He thus approached the Beagle Channel in the Le Maire Strait, which cuts between Cape San Diego, the most southeasterly extremity of Tierra del Fuego, to the west, and the large 50-kilometer wide Isla de los Estados to the east.

Swinging west after clearing Le Maire Channel, HMS *Beagle* would have passed the three islands of Nueva, Picton and Lennox. Could Darwin and Captain Fitzroy, one wonders, have imagined that 150 years later in 1979, a conflict between Argentina and Chile over these three forlorn rocky outcrops was only avoided at the last minute by the timely mediation of the Vatican emissary, Cardinal Samore! But all this is part of the fantastic reality of South America that never ceases to astound.

Mysterious Grandeur

Tierra del Fuego, remote, little inhabited and with sparse wildlife, remains today very much as Darwin pictured it: "Tierra del Fuego may be described as a mountainous land, partly submerged in the sea, so that deep bays and inlets occupy the place where valleys should exist. The mountain sides, except on the exposed western coast, are covered from the water's edge upwards by one great forest. The trees reach to an elevation of between 1,000 and 1,500 feet, and are succeeded by a band of peat, with minute alpine plants; and this again is succeeded by a line of perpetual snow."

In 1956 the English painter Edward Seago, subject of an earlier publication by the author, accompanied His Royal Highness Prince Philip, the Duke of Edinburgh, on the royal yacht *Britannia* on an extensive four-month voyage which included passing through the Le Maire Strait en route to Grahamland. While in this inhospitable South Atlantic area, Edward Seago captured admirably the drama of the majestic terrain which Darwin had described so aptly 120 years earlier. "I was astonished," Darwin writes, ". . . when I first saw a range . . . with every valley filled with streams of ice descending to the sea coast. Almost every arm of the sea, which penetrates to the interior higher chain, not only in Tierra del Fuego, but on the coast for 650 miles northwards, is terminated by 'tremendous and astonishing glaciers' as described by one of the officers on the survey. Great masses of ice frequently fall from these icy cliffs, and the crash reverberates like the broadside of a man-of-war through the lonely channels."

Indians of Tierra del Fuego

The Fuegian Indians, whose only garment consisted of "a mantle made of guanaco skin, with the wool outside," impressed Darwin very little. "I could not have believed how wide was the difference between savage and civilized man," he commented, on observing their abject manner, evident lack of socio-political leadership and their speech, which consisted merely of "hoarse, guttural and clicking sounds." In one group of four men, an old man, the spokesman and evident head of the family, "had a fillet of white feathers tied round his head, which partly confined his black coarse and entangled hair. His face was crossed by two broad transverse parallel bars; one painted bright red, reached form ear to ear and included the upper lip; the other, white like chalk, extended above and parallel to the first, so that even his eyelids were thus colored."

They provided, however, some evident humorous interludes. Darwin recounts that when they saw the white arms of the officers, they apparently "mistook two or three of the officers, who were rather shorter and fairer, though adorned with large beards, for the ladies of our party!"

Rubén Darió's *A Colón*

How different, indeed, were these forlorn Indians of Tierra del Fuego, whose lives had probably changed little in a thousand years, from those earlier magnificent peoples further to the north—the Incas of Peru and the Aztecs of Mexico, whom the early 20th-century Nicaraguan romantic Rubén Darió had idealized in some famous lines: "The Indians were proud, loyal and naïve, their heads embellished with feather headdresses. If only the white men had been like Atahualpa and Montezuma!"

Ushuaia

If Darwin had been able to sail along the Beagle Channel now, he would have found no changes in the magnificent vistas, the sunsets would be as eternally breathtaking, and the timid and elusive Patagonian foxes would still move furtively through the trees. But the Indians would virtually have disappeared and there, along the southern shores of Tierra del Fuego, he would have been surprised to encounter a notable sign of progress, the bustling and dynamic port of Ushuaia, Argentina's southernmost settlement and a colorful introduction to a remarkable country.

The elusive Patagonian fox continues to roam the wooded landscape, a destiny not shared by the Falkland's Warrah fox, which Darwin saw living in great numbers but which became extinct when the last one was killed at Shallow Bay, West Falklands, in 1876.

Jumping Orca whale.

A softly glowing moon casts a limpid light against a roseate sky just before sunset in the southern Chilean fjords.

Towering ice-blue spires lend scale and immensity to this glacier scene in southern Chile.

The waterfront of Port Stanley, capital of the islands called Falklands by the British and Malvinas by the Argentines.

In front of Port Stanley's Anglican Cathedral, a giant whalebone juxtaposed with lupins and hollyhocks—
flowers commonly found in English gardens—underlines the ties of south Atlantic Kelpers to a world more than 8,000 miles away.

Victorian-style town houses in Port Stanley suggest the orderly tidiness of English suburbs.

Greenhouses in the British Governor's residence in Port Stanley allows horticulture to flourish despite inclement weather.

The Port Stanley waterfront obelisk commemorates the heroic but little known 1914 battle of the Falklands between British and German warships.

Plaque beside the 1914 monument reveals that the loss of life in the Anglo-German naval confrontation at the start of the First World War was more than that of the 1982 war between the United Kingdom and Argentina.

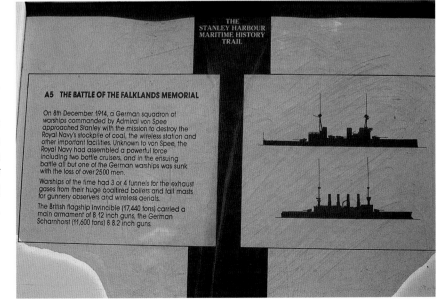

THE
STANLEY HARBOUR
MARITIME HISTORY
TRAIL

A5   THE BATTLE OF THE FALKLANDS MEMORIAL

On 8th December 1914, a German squadron of warships commanded by Admiral von Spee approached Stanley with the mission to destroy the Royal Navy's stockpile of coal, the wireless station and other important facilities. Unknown to von Spee, the Royal Navy had assembled a powerful force including two battle cruisers, and in the ensuing battle all but one of the German warships was sunk with the loss of over 2500 men.

Warships of the time had 3 or 4 funnels for the exhaust gases from their huge coalfired boilers and tall masts for gunnery observers and wireless aerials.

The British flagship Invincible (17,440 tons) carried a main armament of 8 12 inch guns, the German Scharnhorst (11,600 tons) 8 8.2 inch guns.

Port Stanley Museum curator John Smith stands proudly beside a 19th-century symphonion, badly damaged during the 1982 Falklands War but subsequently restored.

A stark and simple monument expresses the gratitude of the islanders to the British forces who brought the 1982 conflict between Argentina and the United Kingdom to an end.

IN MEMORY OF
THOSE WHO
LIBERATED US

14 JUNE 1982

With windows looking out onto a village green graced by commemorative artillery and a ship's mast, the Upland Goose Hotel, originally named in 1871 the Eagle Inn and subsequently the Ship Hotel, continues the congenial traditions of its predecessors.

Falkland beauty Ellaline Terriss (1871–1971), toast of the Edwardian era,
is remembered in the Port Stanley Museum.

Glacier in the Beagle Channel, as Darwin would have seen it.

Landscape near the Le Maire Strait, south Atlantic. Oil painting by English artist Edward Seago (1910–74).

CHAPTER VI

Argentina: From Ushuaia and Iguazú to Cosmopolitan Buenos Aires, South America's Most European City

Incredible Argentina

The traveler who first experiences Argentina in Ushuaia will be surprised. Here among breathtaking scenic vistas is a city that is "new"—in the sense that most of its development has occurred in the last 30 years of the 20th century, but which yet has about it something of a frontier port environment. This is, however, just one aspect of the astonishing variety of Argentina, a mere introduction to the spectacular topography, boundless resources and exuberant élan of this incredible country. Its spellbinding mood can best be experienced in a lightning voyage of close to 4,000 kilometers—from Ushuaia's lakes, glaciers and mountains north to Buenos Aires, South America's most Latin and least Latin American city, and then northeast to the sultry jungle surroundings of the mighty Iguazú Falls.

Ushuaia: The Port "At the End of the World"

Ushuaia, the world's most southern port, is the capital of Tierra del Fuego. Located about 19 kilometers from the Chilean border and about 520 kilometers from Port Stanley, capital of the Falkland Islands, the port lies at the eastern end of the Beagle Channel. A ship sailing south from the Atlantic through the Strait of Magellan will reach Ushuaia by turning to the east when the Strait intersects the Beagle Channel.

This is a land of dramatic vistas. Ushuaia nestles beneath the towering Five Brothers mountains, whose snow-capped peaks are bathed in soft golden tints in the crepuscular glow of early evening. The light here, indeed, can be breathtaking, especially when the sun coming out after rain illuminates in vivid hues the yellow hulls of ships in the harbor against a lowering gray sky. Many of these vessels catch the huge *centollas*, local crabs that are Ushuaia's gourmet delicacy.

The architecture is picturesque, albeit somewhat haphazard in style. Some of the buildings, like the old penitentiary that once housed political prisoners, are of stone and brick; it is now a well appointed museum, which shares local historical honors with the aptly titled Museum of the End of the World. Other structures, of wood, favor a colorful geometry of upright triangular shapes.

Ushuaia's rapid development in the 1980s and 1990s is due almost entirely to its scenic attractions. Among them

is a small glacier up in the mountains near the town, reachable by a cable car that travels over woods, fields and a boulder-strewn brook. For the traveler with more time to spare, there are the Tierra del Fuego National Park, Lakes Kami and Fagnano and Estancia Harberton, a vast 50,000-acre ranch of woods and marshes given in the 19th century by the Argentine government to Thomas Bridges in recognition of his accomplishments.

Sharing center stage with Rudolf Valentino and Tino Rossi as the Latin idol of the years between the two World Wars, the singer Carlos Gardel was born in France in the late 19th century and tragically killed in an air crash in 1935. His charismatic personality and voice endowed the tango with a new sense of romantic passion in such famous songs as Caminito *(a small street in Buenos Aires in the old Italian port section of La Boca) and* Mi Buenos Aires Querido *(The Buenos Aires I Love).*

From Ushuaia it is 2,000 kilometers north to a very different *ambiente*, or atmosphere: that of South America's most cosmopolitan city, Buenos Aires.

Mi Buenos Aires Querido

Mi Buenos Aires Querido is the title of a lilting tango by Carlos Gardel, enduring idol of the 1930s, and it does a lot to explain why Argentines are so proud of their remarkable city, founded in 1680 by Pedro de Mendoza.

Several things are immediately noticeable about Buenos Aires. It is, first of all, South America's most Latin, and least Latin American city—a distinction due to its unmistakable European patina. Secondly, it's a relatively new city, owing its elegance, wide avenues and *belle époque* architecture to the transformation of the old city that began in the 1870s. Thirdly, Buenos Aires has been the fulcrum of cultural activity defining a distinctly Argentine cultural and intellectual character. Finally, it has been the focal point of government: the city where Juan Domingo Perón first mobilized the *descamisado* shirtless workers in the 1940s and where, until the early 1980s, military *golpe de estado* takeovers ushered in military rule.

There are constant reminders that, unlike the more indigenous capitals of other Latin American countries, Buenos Aires, even more so than Montevideo or Santiago, is very European. It is primarily a blend of Spanish and Italian people, French architecture and English traditions, which extend from the railroads to sporting activities and institutions like three-piece suits, Hotel Claridge and the Bristol Tea Room. The country is also drawn to popular U.S. fads, whether in hi-tech, fast-food consumption or entertainment.

On the vast pampa of Buenos Aires province, along the northern borders with Bolivia, Paraguay and Brazil, and to the west along the Andean border with Chile, a certain European influence is also in evidence. You notice it in such places as vineyards in the wine country around Mendoza, and in the Jesuit missions which extend both northeast and northwest from Córdoba. But external influences are more diluted here. Notable pre-Columbian Indian cultures in such areas as the Calchaqui Valley between Tucumán and Salta in the northwest have left a significant heritage which has nothing to do with later European arrivals.

Two Notable Plazas Reflect Distinguished Historical Origins

Plaza San Martín and Plaza de Mayo, the two most eminent plazas of Buenos Aires, are named respectively in honor of the country's national hero and the revolutionary Argentina uprising of May 1810 against Spanish control. Plaza San Martín under shady trees has a more rustic and relaxed atmosphere and is a good place to start; in contrast the few palm trees in the more open Plaza de Mayo are surrounded by the nation's seats of political, military and religious authority.

General José de San Martín, Argentine national hero and protagonist of the early 19th-century independence movement.

Plaza San Martín

From the port area where cruise liners normally dock, it's no more than a 800-meter walk to Plaza San Martín. En route one passes the square named in honor of the Argentine Air Force's fine performance in the 1982 Malvinas/Falklands war, in the center of which is the Torre de los Ingleses or the English Tower. An imposing tall redbrick clock tower vaguely reminiscent of London's Big Ben, it faces ornate Retiro, the city's main railroad station. The latter two edifices are reminiscent of the markedly English atmosphere at the turn of the century, when Buenos Aires was the hub for primary products reaching the city by rail for shipment overseas.

Remembering the 1982 War

The first point of interest in Plaza San Martín, the Islas Malvinas Memorial is an austere semicircular structure with the names of the more than 600 Argentines who died in the brief and ill-fated 1982 War of the Malvinas. About half the total military losses of just under 650 (356 Navy, 4 Naval Air, 35 Marines, 193 Army and 54 Air Force) occurred when the Argentine cruiser *General Belgrano* was sunk by the British submarine HMS *Conqueror*, resulting in 321 military and two civilian Argentine deaths. Tactical considerations and technical factors had prompted the British War Cabinet in London to authorize the attack on May 2, even though the *Belgrano* was slightly outside the General Exclusion Area of 200 miles which Britain had established around the Falkland Islands.

The somber mood of the Malvinas Monument, recalling a less than illustrious moment in Argentine military history, is dispelled as one climbs the gentle slope of the plaza, shaded by trees including a magnificent *ombu*, towards the statue of General José de San Martín. San Martín, a professional military officer, was more sober in mood than his flamboyant liberator counterpart, Simón Bolívar. San Martín returned to Buenos Aires from London after local national forces had first expelled the British from Buenos Aires in 1806 and 1807, and then rebelled against Spanish control on the celebrated date of May 25, 1810.

While the United Provinces of the Rió de la Plata, the forerunner of present-day Argentina, were declaring their independence from Spain in the northern city of Tucumán in 1816, San Martín was assembling new national military forces in very difficult circumstances. He later led them across the Andes and defeated the Spanish royal forces in Chile at the battle of Chacabuco. San Martín's crossing of the Andes, which rise well above 20,000 feet, stands as a more impressive feat than that of Napoleon crossing of the 13,000-foot high Alps. San Martín also accomplished this feat without the strong logistical support which the French army enjoyed.

The triumph at Chacabuco paved the way for San Martín to move north to Peru to link up with Bolívar. A self-sacrificing man who eschewed political ambition, he later made the momentous decision, when he joined Bolivar in the famed meeting at Ecuador's port of Guayaquil, to step aside and leave the Venezuelan in charge. San Martín not only recognized the need for a sole commander-in-chief, but also disagreed with Bolívar on Peru's future. San Martín favored a nationalist monarchy to replace Spanish rule, while Bolívar sought a constitutional republic.

San Martín's monument is adjacent to two notable buildings, both from the turn of the century: the mansion of the prominent Anchorena family, and the Argentine Army Círculo Militar Officers Club. The latter's imposing exterior and ornate interior—a frequent site of official receptions for the author during his military attaché assignment at the U.S. Embassy in the early 1970s—is an indication of the prestige enjoyed by the Argentine army until its lackluster performance against the British in 1982.

Museo Fernandez Blanco: Reliving the Colonial Era

From here, a leisurely stroll down Avenida Santa Fé to Calle Suipacha brings one to the Museo Isaac Fernandez Blanco, a handsome edifice with gracious gardens evoking the era of Spanish colonial rule. It is arguably one of South

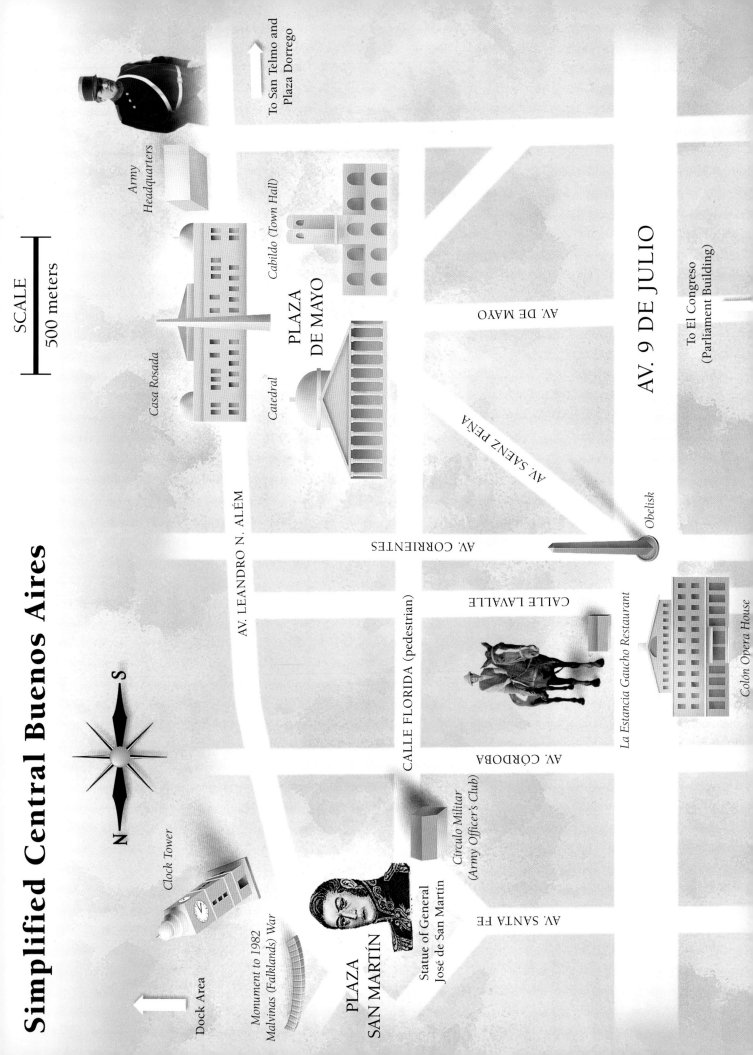

Simplified Central Buenos Aires

SCALE
500 meters

N — S

Dock Area

Clock Tower

Monument to 1982
Malvinas (Falklands) War

PLAZA
SAN MARTÍN

Statue of General
José de San Martín

Círculo Militar
(Army Officer's Club)

Army
Headquarters

To San Telmo and
Plaza Dorrego

Casa Rosada

Cabildo (Town Hall)

Catedral

PLAZA
DE MAYO

AV. LEANDRO N. ALÉM

CALLE FLORIDA (pedestrian)

CALLE LAVALLE

AV. CÓRDOBA

AV. SANTA FE

La Estancia Gaucho Restaurant

Colón Opera House

AV. CORRIENTES

Obelisk

AV. DE MAYO

AV. SAENZ PEÑA

AV. 9 DE JULIO

To El Congreso
(Parliament Building)

America's most pleasant environment in which to view secular and religious paintings, wood carvings, *bargueños* (wood cabinets with drawers), period furniture, silverwork and costumes dating from the late 17th to the 19th century.

Plaza de Mayo

As the Simplified Map of Central Buenos Aires illustrates, it is less than two kilometers' walk along Calle Florida to the second major city square, Plaza de Mayo. In the 1970s, a stroll down pedestrian Calle Florida was a pleasant interlude amid art galleries and upscale stores, but those days have gone. The top quality establishments have shifted over to the areas around Avenidas Santa Fé and Alvear, and Calle Florida, apart from its attractive Galeriá Pacífica shopping arcade, is a pale shadow of its former self.

Plaza de Mayo is flat and open, unlike the gently sloping and tree-shaded Plaza San Martín, so the vistas are more spacious. The view from the west end is especially noteworthy. To the right is the two-story, gracefully arched Cabildo, the old Town Hall dating from approximately 1750. On the left the Catedral, the Metropolitan Cathedral, with a neoclassical facade of pediment, entablature, capitals and columns that date from 1827, is San Martín's burial site. He had left Buenos Aires for the last time in 1829 for exile in France and died in Europe, and his body was subsequently brought back to Argentina.

The Plaza has fountains, brightly hued flower beds, lots of pigeons, a small central obelisk, an equestrian statue and behind it, at the east end, the seat of government called the Casa Rosada, or Pink House. An immediately appealing building in soft pastel tones, it provided the balcony from which President Juan Domingo Perón, twice elected President in 1946 and 1952, used his charismatic populism to harangue the city's working masses until he was removed from power in 1955 by a military coup.

It's perhaps no coincidence that, only a few hundred meters behind the Casa Rosada, the Argentine Army headquarters is located in a monumental edifice often referred to as "The White Elephant." Throughout this century, the Argentine military frequently intervened in the political arena, claiming a tutelary role as the guardian of traditional sovereignty. Since this tradition was synonymous with the predominant political role of a landed *terrateniente* oligarchical elite tied to foreign capital and to uncontrollable fluctuations in the international commodities market, the Argentine military became identified with a conservative, status quo nationalism.

As Labor Minister in 1945, Colonel Perón was different. He wanted a new Argentina that was more autonomous and industrialized, and in which the urban workers would have a stake. Yet Perón was not a leftist. Rather, he was closer in thinking to fascism, although it was a fascism with its own Argentine imprimatur, rather than that of the corporativist state of Mussolini's Italy, where he was briefly assigned in the 1930s. The fact that Argentina provided sanctuary in the post-war years to certain Nazis, of which Adolf Eichmann was the most prominent, has tended to reinforce the impression that certain elements in Argentina were sympathetic to the Axis in World War II.

Perón did indeed transform the economic landscape, with his extraordinary wife Eva, a small-town coquette who reinvented herself as a dynamic political figure of major dimensions. But for many Argentines, including the military, the rise of Labor was unpalatable, especially when coupled with the anti-clerical outbursts and burning of churches in 1955. This looked too much like events that preceded the start of the Spanish Civil War in 1936, and a military confrontation between conservative Azules and pro-Peronist Colorados ended with Perón's removal from power and exile in 1955.

By the early 1960s civilian rule was back, but only briefly, and by 1964 General Onganiá had seized power. The U.S. Congress responded with the Conte/Long Amendment, forbidding the sale of sophisticated weaponry to countries with *de facto* military rulers. But the military stayed in charge, albeit with presidents who changed with lightning speed! During the author's military assignment in Argentina from 1969 to 1972, he met with three military Presidents: General Onganiá; General Levingston, who replaced Onganiá; and General Lanusse, who replaced Levingston.

Perón came back in 1974 from exile in Spain, but his death shortly after brought his ineffectual second wife, Isabelita, to power. As the left-wing terrorism of such groups as the Montoneros and Ejército Revolucionario del Pueblo grew, the military expelled Isabela Perón in a *golpe* or *coup d'etat*, a move that ushered in the presidencies of Generals Bignone, Videla, Viola and Galtieri.

It was during these years that the military found themselves involved in *La Guerra Sucia*, the "Dirty War" whose resultant death toll of between 10,000 and 15,000 *desaparecidos* (the disappeared) is still commemorated once weekly in front of the Casa Rosada by the "Mothers of the Plaza de Mayo." It is clear that, in those years, the Argentine military exceeded their authority on many occasions, and equally certain that there were lamentable cases of sadistic brutality. But this indictment does not tell the true story. The left-wing terrorists, ruthless and uncompromising, struck effectively at will against defenseless targets unable to distinguish adversaries who never wore distinctive uniforms. Failure to wear such uniforms, in effect, disqualified the terrorists from treatment as bona fide military prisoners of war under the Geneva Convention.

Secondly, the Argentine middle class, to whom communism was anathema, was inclined to view the military as protectors of the traditional way of life against a potentially rising left-wing tide. In retrospect, that middle class may now be critical of past military rule; but at the time there was a tendency on the part of many people, admittedly without knowing all the facts, to acquiesce tacitly in the ramifications of military *de facto* rule.

The irony is that when General Galtieri and the military did finally fall irrevocably from power in 1982, it was not because of civil rights abuses, but because of their incompetent mismanagement and disastrous strategic errors in the Malvinas/Falklands War with England!

Near the military headquarters, the old Bohemian *barrio* of San Telmo offers a nice contrast in mood. San Telmo is the site of both authentic tango haunts like the Viejo Almacén, as well as of tango shows glamorized in spectacular evening shows. The tango, originating in Germany and then taken up in the late 19th century by Italian and Spanish immigrants who came to be known as Porteños, or residents of the port of Buenos Aires, was originally a spoken medium, accompanied by music, to convey such emotions as nostalgia, longing, betrayal and unrequited love. By the 1920s and 1930s, however, the tango assumed new dimensions as, with the advent of Carlos Gardel, it came to signify passion expressed in both dance and music. Gardel's most famous songs—*Mi Buenos Aires Querido* (*The Buenos Aires I love*), *Caminito* (a street in the old Boca Italian dockside area), and *Volver* (*To Return*) elicit the same romantic responses among many people today as they did before his tragic death in an air crash in 1935.

On Sunday, San Telmo's Plaza Dorrego puts on a highly sophisticated and frequently very costly flea market. It is a colorful, picturesque plaza and there are always some bargains. However, reputable antique dealers are always present, with upscale European antiques at regular prices. Still, if one wants to lay out thousands of dollars for a Louis XVI clock, this is as good a place as any to do it.

From San Telmo, a third interesting segment of Buenos Aires takes in Avenida 9 de Julio, the world's widest urban thoroughfare, and its nearby sights—the Congreso Parliament Building, five blocks west of 9 de Julio on Avenida de Mayo, the Obelisk in the middle of 9 de Julio and the celebrated Colón Opera House.

The Congress

Looking somewhat like the Invalides in Paris and the Capitol in Washington, the eye-catching Congreso, completed in 1906, boasts an Italianate dome and neoclassical Greek facade. The plaza in front of the building is a delight, as is the Monumento a los Dos Congresos, a handsome and very photogenic sculptural ensemble that includes that omnipresent South American icon, a spectacular condor with outspread wings. Its abode, the High Andes mountains, is symbolized by the granite steps leading up to the monument, which commemorates the epic independence events of 1810 and 1816, as well as the 1813 abolition of slavery.

Avenida Nueve de Julio, World's Widest Avenue

The immense width of Avenida 9 de Julio is a reminder that Buenos Aires is a city dating from the late 19th century, when Baron Haussman remodeled Paris and made the Arc de Triomphe the hub of broad radiating avenues. The builders of Avenida 9 de Julio echoed these urban planning concepts, making the soaring Obelisk in the middle of the Avenue's Plaza de la República their landmark *par excellence*.

The Colón Opera House

Only three blocks west along 9 de Julio is the Colón Opera House, the apotheosis of Buenos Aires cultural life and of the much vaunted Porteño claim to living in South America's most civilized city. The Teatro Colón was fittingly inaugurated, in 1908, with Giuseppe Verdi's *Aida*, and since then has hosted the world's greatest figures of opera and ballet. Although the Colón faces onto Avenida 9 de Julio, the entrance is on the other side, in the charming Plaza Lavalle, whose fountains and statuary include the pirouettes of skillfully sculpted bronze ballet dancers.

By the time you're ready for lunch, there are endless alternatives. Argentines like to eat well and, for a superb *bife de lomo con ensalada de berro*—a tender steak with watercress salad—in a colorful gaucho setting, the author's favorite place for 30 years has been La Estancia, on Calle Lavalle, barely two blocks away from the Obelisk.

Fashion Chic in Avenida Alvear

From the Obelisk down 9 de Julio, across Santa Fé and over to the Museum of Fine Arts is a good walk of about three kilometers through much of upscale Buenos Aires. The Museo Nacional de Bellas Artes has superb European holdings, from Rembrandt van Rijn up to the French Impressionists and Symbolists, as well as such important 20th-century figures as Vuillard, Bonnard and Modigliani. At the same time, one can see how Argentine artists have both assimilated European influences and also developed original autonomous styles with highly personal forms of expression. Major figures are Pettoruti, Castagnino, Spilimbergo, Soldi, Berni. Seguí, Quinquelo Martin, Fridman and Kuitca.

If the Fine Arts Museum tells one a lot about the Argentine cultural *gestalt*, the Recoleta, the vast funerary emporium that is reached by a short stroll up a grassy slope, provides trenchant insight into Argentine elitism. Many of the great

The author's sketch of a detail of a brilliantly colored painting by Emilio Pettoruti shows how the 20th-century Argentine artist assimilated, exploited and interpreted in his individual manner the iconography and structural design of French analytical and synthetic cubism.

Born in 1929 in the provincial pueblo of Los Toldos to an unmarried mother whose admirer, a married man who lived nearby, Eva Duarte went to Buenos Aires at 16 to escape the monotony of small-town life. A vivacious coquette, she became a radio announcer whose subsequent marriage to Colonel Juan Domingo Perón would change not only her life, but also that of Argentina.

With Perón's election to the presidency in 1946, Eva Duarte de Perón turned her attention to the formation of a Woman's Peronist Party, workers' rights and public welfare. With a charisma that was almost demagogic, she frequently harangued Porteño urban workers. "If the people ask for my life," she once said, "I would give it singing, because the happiness of one descamisado (shirtless one) is worth more than my life."

political, literary, military, and educational figures have been buried here, and their names—Mitre, Sarmiento, Aramburu, Avellaneda *et al*—on their resplendent mausolea testify to their privileged place in Argentine history, and to their will to perpetuate their distinction in death as much as in life. It's ostentatious, but impressive nevertheless, especially as some of the structures are beautifully made. One striking exception is a modest tomb in the Duarte family burial lot: that of the remarkable Eva Perón, buried nine meters underground in an inaccessible vault.

Eva Perón: From Coquette to Charismatic Populist

Eva Perón was hardly a welcome addition to this domain of blue-bloods, and the inaccessibility of her tomb suggests an apprehension, at the time, that her body—which had undergone a bizarre series of mysterious voyages to Italy and Spain since her untimely death in 1952 at only age 33—might be unceremoniously removed. However, she did better than her husband. President Juan Perón's body lies on the outskirts of Buenos Aires in the modest Chacarita cemetery, as well known for his presence as it has always been famed for containing the body of the 1930s tango idol Carlos Gardel.

Both Eva Perón and her husband Juan D. Perón have always been controversial figures in Argentine life, and understandably so. Their emphasis upon the rights of urban workers in the 1940s and 1950s was a direct challenge to the conservative *terrateniente* landholding class, whose great *estancias*, or ranches, had made Argentina by the 1930s the world's fifth wealthiest nation.

The Peróns were as eulogized by their constituency, the *descamisados* or shirtless workers, as they were excoriated by the nation's traditionally conservative elite. It is not difficult to see why. To jolt Argentina into the realities of 20th century socio-economic life, the Peróns often resorted to using autocratic methods in a frequently highly charged, charismatic populist framework.

The elegant Alvear Palace Hotel, a few hundred meters from the entrance to the Recoleta and the adjacent Pilar Convent, and graced by colorful flags of foreign nations, was precisely the sort of place where "establishment" detractors of the Peróns would have gathered. Its refined ambiance, including a striking hall of mirrors on the ground floor, is an ideal spot for dignified repose, accompanied by a glass of one of the many superb Argentine wines, like the fruity Torrontes Viejo white wine from Salta. This is a favorite place for the *haut monde* of elegant Buenos Aires society to meet for a drink, the upscale designer stores on Avenida Alvear testifying to the Argentine penchant for panache, flair and style.

All this is part of living well in Argentina, but the Argentines also know how to be a sentimental, sensitive and compassionate people. During the 1970s, when John Davis Lodge was U.S. Ambassador to Argentina, his elegant wife Francesca was famed for raising money for charity by putting on spectacular fashion shows, which brought the country's top models to the U.S. Embassy, and which were strongly supported by Argentine society.

Flair, Style and Panache

Avenida Alvear is one of the best places to show that the Argentines have a very special sense of style as far as personal appearance is concerned. It is full of the finest international and Argentine clothes and accessories. Looking good is a *sine qua non* of Porteño life, whether in fashionable attire or in physical appearance, as two local words, *facha* and *pinta*, the *lunfardo* or slang for "looks," signify. It has in fact been estimated that on a percentage basis far more Argentines than North Americans undergo facial surgery; and, whether it is President Saul Meném or a young girl, Argentines make no secrecy of the fact that they are proud of having given themselves new facial features!

An Illustrious Literary Tradition

They are also proud of being voracious readers of every imaginable type of publication. One has only to look at the numerous *kioskos*, newspaper stands that are in profusion everywhere, to realize how amazingly eclectic Argentine reading interests are. And newsstand sales are a day and night proposition; it's not unusual to find well-dressed people thumbing through literary, fashion, political or art magazines in the early hours of the morning.

Argentine enthusiasm for the printed word reflects a virtuoso literary tradition. Since José Hernandez produced his classic gaucho work *Martin Fierro*, literary talents have proliferated in the 20th century. They include José Luis Borges, one of the world's greatest tellers of short stories, Julio Cortazar, Eduardo Mallea, Manuel Puig and Ernesto Sábato. Although best known for his famed *Sobre Héroes y Tumbas* (*About Heroes and Tombs*), Sabato is perhaps at his best in *El Túnel* (*The Tunnel*), an incisive story set in modern Buenos Aires in which a painter describes how he kills his mistress. The novel's philosophical impact is the focus on the anomy of the big city, and the dilemma of people who are unable to communicate with one another.

Palermo, Belgrano and Tigre

There is a magnificent old *ombu* tree in the small park across from the Café de la Paix, but if one wants the tranquility of parks and lakes, the city's northern Palermo area is the place to go. It's no more than four kilometers from the Recoleta Cemetery, and reached either on spacious Avenida Libertador, or by the longer waterfront Costanera, a stretch of lively restaurants and nightspots strung out along the Rió de la Plata. Both approaches bring you into Palermo via the traffic circle dominated by the striking Monument to the Spaniards. Nearby are the Zoo, the Rosedal Park with a lake for boating, the U.S. Embassy that looks onto a park with a statue of Franklin Roosevelt, and the palatial U.S. Ambassador's residence, an early 1900s mansion covering, together with its garden and grounds, an entire city block. Nearby is the site of the annual *Rural*—a famous traditional annual commercial and social spectacle whose gaucho riding displays and exhibits of Aberdeen Angus cattle are some of the attractions that honor the Argentine rural life of the *campo*.

Much of Palermo is very evocative of the ambiance, people and architecture of a European city. The Hipódromo race-course, polo fields and, in the neighboring Belgrano, white-flanneled cricketers are as much a legacy of 19th- and early 20th-century English influence as is the local golf.

Such northern suburbs as Vicente Lopez, Acassuso, Olivos, with their stately mansions behind high walls, are very much the place to live and a popular site of *asados*—the Argentine equivalent for a barbecue—on lazy weekend afternoons. Beyond these suburbs is the riverside suburb of Tigre, at the confluence of the Lujan and Tigre Rivers, the point from which everything from small craft to large cabin cruisers make their way through the generally muddy brown waters of the many channels making up the approximately 2,000 kilometers of the Paraná River delta.

The most interesting place to visit in the Tigre area is the Island of Martín Garciá, whose colorful past includes European colonial rivalries, a major naval battle in the early 19th-century independence struggle against Spain, and a 20th-century role as a penal colony. Three Argentine Presidents—Irigoyen, Alvear and Frondizi—were imprisoned here, as was Colonel Juan D. Perón in 1945, shortly before he was elected to the presidency of Argentina in 1946.

A cruise from Tigre is a sudden change from the nearby urban metropolis of Buenos Aires, a gentle metamorphosis to a more Arcadian setting. For a truly dramatic change, however, and the opportunity to contemplate the transcendental majesty of nature in a tropical jungle setting, one needs to go to the northeast—to the Brazilian border and to the monumental Falls of Iguazú.

The Wonders of Iguazú

The Iguazú Falls, known as the Cataratas de Iguazú in Argentina, and Foz da Iguacu in Brazil, are located on the Argentine/Brazilian border, approximately 1,000 kilometers northeast of Buenos Aires and 1,100 kilometers southwest of Rió de Janeiro.

Each side offers spectacular, albeit different views and impressions. From Argentina's superb Hotel de Cataratas, a path through tropical vegetation leads to the first of many falls one mile away. The magic is immediate: here in a luxuriant jungle terrain

Coatis at Iguazú Falls: these cuddlesome long-snouted mammals of the South American jungle are similar in size, fur patterning and color to the North American raccoon.

of brilliantly colored orchids, the thunderous roar of the water, the mists rising in diaphanous veils and the sun glinting on the falling cascades are the apotheosis of nature's majesty. Here, in a luxuriant jungle setting, is a direct dialogue with a primeval world, especially apparent as the first rays of morning sunlight illuminate the Falls. The only interruption may be the sudden appearance of friendly coatis, genial raccoon-like animals pleasantly untroubled by the presence of humans in their domain.

When the Spanish explorer Alvar Nuñez Cabeza de Vaca stumbled upon the Falls in 1541, it must have been an astonishing experience. For here was the majesty of nature at its most sublime: clouds of mists swirling 500 feet upwards, 275 separate falls or cataracts (that increase to about 350 in the rainy season) with heights of between 200 and 269 feet, and the whole spectacular ensemble spread out over two and a half miles.

"Iguazú," the Guarani Indian word signifying "Great Water," must indeed have seemed an appropriate name, if only because of the monumental flow of water. During the rainy season the rate of flow, normally calculated at about 62,000 cubic feet per second, can increase to a phenomenal 450,000 cubic feet per second! And there are amazing individual falls: the 500-foot wide *Garganta del Diablo*, or Devil's Throat, for example, whose roaring tons of swirling water plunge vertiginously down into a terrifying devil's inferno. Comparison of Iguazú with Victoria and Niagara Falls is illuminating. Iguazú's overall width of just over 13,000 feet is twice that of Victoria's, thirteen times that of the 1,000-foot width of the U.S side of Niagara, and about five times the width of the 2,600-foot long curving crest on the Canadian side. Iguazú's average 235-foot height of fall of water is less than that of Victoria's 355 feet, and greater than Niagara's 162 feet. Victoria's greater height creates a mist that rises to 1,000 feet, twice that of Iguazú's 500 feet.

The savage wildness, untrammeled majesty and sublime aura of Iguazú is a disconcerting metamorphosis from the sophisticated urban cosmopolitanism of Buenos Aires. Yet the pulsing rhythm of the vast Argentine metropolis, which ranks with Sydney as the world's most exciting southern capital city, sets a standard that is unique in South America. One smaller city in the Rió de la Plata region, however, has much about it that is similar in terms of history, mood, ethnic makeup and cultural ambiance. This is Montevideo, capital of Uruguay, located a mere 200 kilometers to the east across the river.

Sunlit Ushuaia, Argentina's most southern port, with lofty shadowed peaks behind.

The Argentine flag flutters between a mass of white marguerites and Ushuaia's geometric wooden architecture.

At the base of Ushuaia Glacier, the author is photographed with a group of young Argentines on a holiday outing.

(Right) Cablecar takes visitors up to Ushuaia Glacier above mountain firs and a rippling, boulder-strewn brook.

(Below) Symbol of a sinister past, the Ushuaia Penitentiary, now restored as a museum, provides insight into this once remote outpost's history.

In Buenos Aires' Plaza San Martín, the statue of 19th-century writer Esteban Echeverría stands near the patrician Marriott-Plaza Hotel.

The famous Clocktower, near to the Sheraton Hotel and Argentine Air Force headquarters, is a reminder of English influence in Argentina's past.

Two soldiers mount solemn guard in Plaza de Mayo in front of the austere semicircular monument honouring Argentina's dead in the 1982 War of the Malvinas (the Argentine name for the Falkland Islands).

Statue of Argentine national hero General José de San Martín is the traditional place for the ceremonial laying of floral wreaths by the diplomatic corps and distinguished visitors.

Unlike the tree-shaded Plaza San Martín, Buenos Aires' second great square Plaza de Mayo provides a spacious open setting. Facing it is the Casa Rosada (presidential "Pink House"), seen in the background behind an equestrian statue.

The handsome equestrian statue in front of the imposing facade of the entrance to the Casa Rosada symbolizes the role in South American history of the caudillo or military leader on horseback..

*Behind fragrant purple jacaranda and beds of cheerful yellow flowers, the arched white Cabildo,
the Town Hall, faces the Casa Rosada across the Plaza de Mayo.*

*No more than 500 meters behind the Casa Rosada, the looming army headquarters,
nicknamed "The White Elephant," rises ominously as a reminder of the military's presence in Argentina's political past.*

The Congreso Parliament building, in late 19th-century neoclassical style.

Set in front of the Congreso Parliament building, this figure of the condor, with its vast wings, is suggestive of the freedom guaranteed by parliamentary democracy.

This obelisk, a famed Buenos Aires landmark, rears upward from the center of Avenida 9 de Julio, the world's widest urban thoroughfare.

The Colón Opera House, with decorative ceiling by Argentine painter Soldi, highlights Argentine ties to Europe and reinforces Porteño claims that Buenos Aires is South America's most cultured city.

In the plaza in front of the Opera House, the pirouettes of bronze ballet dancers enliven a city fountain.

Tango dancers. Characterized by long gliding steps and sudden pauses, the tango is one of Latin America's most spectacular dances which is now enjoying a popular revival worldwide.

Detail from "Más Allá de la Noche" by Liber Fridman. Using a combination of mixed media, the painter conjures up the mysteries of a bygone world as an owl and human figure fly through magical space.

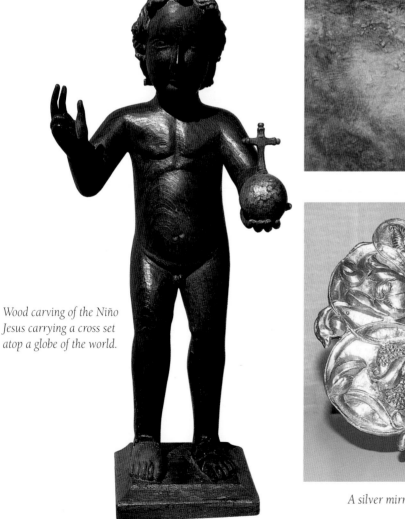

Wood carving of the Niño Jesus carrying a cross set atop a globe of the world.

A silver mirror from 1780 ornately decorated with baroque carvings.

Rembrandt's portrait of his sister Lisbeth in the collection of the National Fine Arts Museum in Buenos Aires.

"Portrait of a Woman" by tragic Italian artist Amadeo Modigliani (1884–1920), in Buenos Aires National Fine Arts Museum.

This 1972 fashion show with the city's top models was arranged to raise funds for charity by Mrs Francesca Lodge (center), wife of the then U.S. Ambassador John Davis Lodge.

Entrance to the Recoleta, South America's most eye-catching cemetery, where many historical figures are interred in magnificent mausolea, and where Eva Perón is buried in a simple tomb nine meters underground.

*On the Argentine side of the Iguazú Falls, roiling water hurtles downward in the
Garganta del Diablo or the Throat of the Devil.*

(Above) Lush jungle vegetation and tropical vistas enhance the spectacle of the Iguazú Falls.

(Below) The immense cascades comprising the Iguazu Falls can be especially well appreciated from the Brazilian side.

Historic Colonia del Sacramento

Fifty kilometers to the north of Buenos Aires across the Rió de la Plata is Colonia del Sacramento, a fitting introduction to the neighboring nation of Uruguay. The port town was founded in 1680 by the Portuguese Manoel Lobo, whose entrepreneurial vision saw its potential as a contraband center that could rival the Spanish trade monopoly in the Rió de la Plata area directed from Buenos Aires.

The Jesuit Dobritzhoffer recounts how, by 1750, "Portuguese ships, laden with English and Dutch wares, and negro slaves . . . crowd to this port . . . and convey the goods to Paraguay, Peru or Chili (Chile)." And he goes on to note that it is "incredible how many million are lost to the Spanish in this forbidden traffic." The negro slaves would come to be a colorful cultural presence in the 18th and 19th centuries, enlivening Montevideo with their festive dances and Candombé rituals; the latter were vividly portrayed by the renowned Uruguayan artist Pedro Figari (1861–1938) in a series of lively paintings.

By 1777, when Spain created the Viceroyalty of Rió de la Plata—the fourth and final of the Viceregal centers through which Madrid governed South America—Colonia had finally fallen firmly under Spanish control; it would remain so until independence from Spain was achieved in the 1820s. Today, it retains the tranquil charm of a provincial town of centuries ago, distinguished by both a Portuguese and Spanish patina.

Historic Old City

From the Puerta de Campo Gateway and the 1811 Plazoleta near to the Calle de los Suspiros (the Street of Sighs or Whispers), it is barely 200 meters to the Faro, the high white lighthouse from whose upper balcony there is a fine view. It amply encompasses the historic old city, which is not very large, not more than a quarter of a mile from the Puerta del Campo to the seafront, along which the Paseo de San Gabriel runs from north to south for about 400 meters. A stroll here is a voyage into another era, past colorful adobe-type houses shrouded by sycamores, down narrow cobblestone streets where the sudden statue of a conquistador glints in the sunlight, and alongside ancient stone battlements.

There is a constant echo of colonial times. The most prominent examples are the 1680 Iglesia Matriz, or Cathedral, the San Francisco Convent and an early 1800s house that was once the residence of Juan Lavalleja. Like Artigas, Lavalleja, leader of the famous 33 patriots in the independence struggle against Spain, and protagonist of the 1823 "Cry for Liberty," is an heroic subject of constant commemoration in Uruguay.

Some of the places of interest are more recent. Near Colonia, at Real de San Carlos, is a bullring dating from the turn of the century, designed to seat 10,000 spectators as part of what now seems an avant-garde recreational and gambling complex . It attracted considerable attention at the time, as the only Plaza de Toros in southern South America. But the government of Battle y Ordoñez banned bullfighting in 1912, and the plaza has languished ever since as a monument to a failed entrepreneurial dream.

Montevideo: Similarities with Buenos Aires

From Colonia, it is 180 kilometers southeast along the Rió de la Plata to Uruguay's capital of Montevideo, which is roughly the same distance east from Buenos Aires across the water. About half the country's population of 3.2 million lives in the capital of Uruguay, a nation whose income is derived mainly from services, especially tourism, industry and, to a lesser degree than in previous years, from ranching and agriculture.

When Magellan sailed along the Rió de la Plata in 1520, a look-out on his ship called out "Montevideu" ("I have seen a mountain") and thereby gave the country's capital its name. Montevideo is in many ways a smaller, more modest and less spectacular version of its neighboring Argentine capital. There are several obvious similarities. Both cities received important infusions of Spanish and Italian immigrants in the late 19th century. Both became wealthy as exporters of wheat, cattle and sheep products when these were lucrative sources of income. In each country, it was the English who built the railroad systems radiating out from the two capital cities. Buenos Aires and Montevideo are both capitals of nations whose Indian and black peoples—the latter never much in evidence in Argentina— diminished notably in numbers after 1900, leaving a largely homogeneous white population. Both cities became important centers of cultural expression in literature, art, theater and music. Finally, both cities are distinguished by a fetching turn-of-the-century neoclassical, *belle époque* style of elegant architecture.

"Little Switzerland"

In the early years of the 20th century, Uruguay enjoyed exceptional prosperity. Largely as the result of the British introduction of Merino sheep, and Hereford and Shorthorn cattle, ranching and its peripheral products expanded notably. In the first two decades of the 20th century, Uruguay achieved fame at another level: as the first social welfare state in South America. Between 1903 and 1912 a remarkable President, José Battle y Ordoñez, initiated such progressive socio-economic measures as farm credits, eight-hour work days, pensions and unemployment compensation. These achievements, remarkable for those years, earned Uruguay the title of "Little Switzerland."

Turbulent 1970s

By the late 1960s the situation had changed drastically. In an increasingly urban and industrialized world, dependence on primary products in such South American nations as Uruguay inevitably affected their capacity for growth and development. As the economy deteriorated, terrorism appeared. The activities of Raúl Sendic's Tupamaros, responsible for the murder of U.S. Embassy agent Dan Mitrione, prompted President Juan Bordaberry, backed by the Uruguayan military, to drastic measures: suspension of the constitution, banning of trade unions and adoption of a tough anti-terrorism stance that lasted from the early 1970s until normal civilian rule was reinstated in the mid-1980s.

Three Plazas: Zabala, Constitución and Independencia

These turbulent events may be put behind one as one explores the charm of the older parts of Montevideo whose parks, late 19th-century architecture and monuments illustrate the nation's development. On the quayside of the main harbor, for example, is the statue of a docker, symbol of the many workers whose sturdy arms and shoulders have traditionally dispatched Uruguayan products overseas.

Nearby is another, very different statue that is a reminder of European affiliations. It is an imposing rendition of the patriot and protagonist of Italian unity in 1870, Giuseppe Garibaldi, who spent the six years from 1842 to 1848 in Uruguay. Climbing the gentle slope to Rincón Street, a right turn takes one to nearby Plaza Zabala. Here yet another statue, this one of the mounted General Zabala, is the focal point of a square flanked by the Taranto Palace.

Zabala Plaza is the first of three plazas in the historic old city center of Montevideo, as shown by the simplified

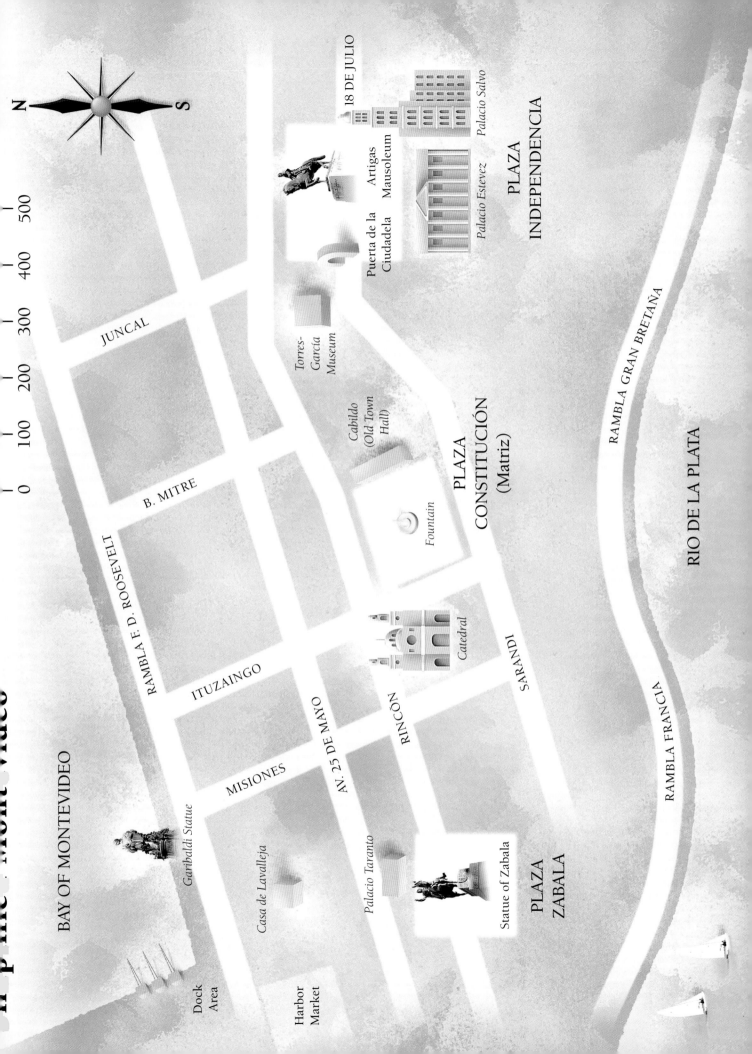

PLAT : Montevideo

N — S

0   100 200 300 400 500

BAY OF MONTEVIDEO

Dock Area

Harbor Market

Garibaldi Statue

Casa de Lavalleja

MISIONES

Palacio Taranto

Statue of Zabala

PLAZA ZABALA

RAMBLA F. D. ROOSEVELT

B. MITRE

ITUZAINGO

AV. 25 DE MAYO

RINCÓN

JUNCAL

Torres-García Museum

Cabildo (Old Town Hall)

Fountain

PLAZA CONSTITUCIÓN (Matriz)

Catedral

SARANDI

Puerta de la Ciudadela

Artigas Mausoleum

18 DE JULIO

Palacio Salvo

Palacio Estevez

PLAZA INDEPENDENCIA

RAMBLA GRAN BRETAÑA

RAMBLA FRANCIA

RIO DE LA PLATA

city map. The distances between these plazas are short—roughly 200 to 300 meters—so they offer the opportunity of a pleasant stroll. Plaza Constitución, a delightful tree-shrouded square, boasts charming outdoor cafés as well as the 1812 stone Cabildo and the 1799 Iglesia Matriz or Cathedral. Designed by the Portuguese architect José de Sá y Fariá, the Cathedral's two striking bell towers face the center of the Plaza, where a graceful fountain with baroque figures is one of the many encomia to the 1823 "Cry for Liberty" of the 33 patriots.

Between Plaza Constitución and Plaza Independencia, on Calle Sarandí, is the Torres-Garciá Museum, a reminder of the remarkable artistic accomplishments of this tiny nation. Joaquín Torres-Garciá (1874–1949) is the most important of an Uruguayan trio of painters of international status, which also includes Juan Manuel Blanes (1830–1901) and the previously mentioned Pedro Figari (1861–1938). Torres-Garciá began as a highly talented realistic painter; however, by the late 1920s he was moving towards the "universal constructivism" for which he was famed. This style included the use of geometricized small pictographs, grouped into frameworks of squares and rectangles to suggest specific meanings and convey an existing aesthetic visual message.

A particular impressive example of his work can be found sculpted on a huge block of stone in the Parque Rodó, adjacent to the Fine Art Museum. To get there one takes the engaging seaside drive, first entitled Rambla Francia and then Rambla Gran Bretaña, that follows the Rió de la Plata along the Malecón (Esplanade) on Montevideo's south side, past the U.S. Embassy.

Torres-Garciá, one of the major artists of the 20th century, was honest in proclaiming his debt to the remarkable pre-Hispanic artistic designs of the ancient Peruvians, as shown in the illustrations on page 154. A famous Torres-Garciá 1930s painting from his famed "five color" style entitled "La Locomotora," when juxtaposed with a superb Nazca textile from about AD 400, suggests parallels between ancient and modern iconographies that are separated by 1,500 years. Major Uruguayan artists influenced by Torres-Garciá were, in the first period, Hector Ragni, Rosa Acle and Amalia Nieto, and in the second period Augusto Torres, Horacio Torres, Julio Alpuy and Gonzalo Fonseca.

Writers and Poets

Although a small nation, Uruguay has produced important literary as well as artistic figures. The poem *Tabare* of the 19th-century writer Juan Zorrilla de San Martín is rightly acclaimed as the apogee of Latin American romantic literature, together with the work of the Nicaraguan essayist and poet Rubén Darió. Probably the best known international writer is Enrique Rodó, who died in 1917, and whose *Ariel* earned fame as a criticism of the materialism of the United States, a nation which at the time he viewed as culturally inferior.

Plaza Independencia

Plaza Independencia is the largest and most striking of Montevideo's plazas, and approaching it from Calle Sarandí takes one through the historically restored Puerta de la Ciudadela. To the left is the Hotel Victoria, whose rooftop café offers a magnificent panoramic view of Montevideo and the port area. To the right is the Palacio Estevez, the national seat of government until 1985, while at the rear rises Montevideo's highest building, originally constructed in 1927 as the Palacio Salvo and now the city's communication tower.

Just off the Plaza to the right is the Solis Theater, with costumes and mock-ups on the second floor detailing the illustrious tradition of an institution which opened in 1856. It hosted such glittering international figures as operatic tenor Enrico Caruso, Russian ballet dancers Pavlova and Nijinsky and French actress Sarah Bernhardt.

Caudillos and Gauchos

In the center of the Plaza rises a fine statue, on a rearing horse, of national hero José Gervasio Artigas, the symbol of the heroic South American *caudillo*. Below the statue is a mausoleum, the perpetually burning flame and honor guard an enduring tribute to his accomplishments and legacy in achieving Uruguayan independence.

The gaucho is a prevalent feature of Uruguayan life, as such articles for sale in Montevideo as the elaborate and costly gaucho belts with silver coins testify. There is also a Museo del Gaucho y de la Moneda, on Avenida 18 de Julio which leads east from Plaza Independencia, and on the same avenue there is a magnificently ornate statue that pays homage to his colorful image.

Museo Municipal de Bellas Artes Juan Manuel Blanes

Perhaps the most poignant tributes of all, however, can be found in the Prado suburb, reached by taking Avenida Libertador General Lavalleja past the monumental neoclassical Legislature Building. They are located in the enchanting Museo Municipal de Bellas Artes Juan Manuel Blanes, an Italianate building which honors the painter of the same name, and whose gardens, statuary and inner patio with fountains evoke the tranquil atmosphere of a rural Roman villa. Inside, there are sensitive renditions of the gaucho by Blanes, as well as his paintings of epic proportions detailing the "Oath of the 33 Patriots" and other salient historical events. The Museum also contains a superb collection of the works of Pedro Figari, many of which are also related to the *campo* or countryside of *estancias* (ranches), fiestas and colorful vegetation.

Punta del Este

Long considered to be South America's most chic summer playground, Punta del Este's fine beaches, pine woods, stately residences and gourmet cuisine attract visitors from all over the world, and especially from Argentina. Some 120 kilometers east of Montevideo, Punta del Este lies south of the town of Maldonado on a peninsula that fronts both the tranquil waters of the Rió de la Plata and the strong Atlantic surf. Justifiably hailed as the pearl of the Uruguayan Riviera, it boasts such additional attractions as a lively artisan market and, six miles offshore, the Isla de Lobos whose colonies of hundreds of thousands of southern fur seals can be visited in small launches.

Uruguay shares the Rió de la Plata with Argentina, and a land border to the north with Brazil. During World War II both Uruguay and Brazil came up briefly against the ramifications of the international conflict. Uruguay witnessed the dramatic scuttling of the German *Graf Spee* off Montevideo, but Brazil's involvement was to be a direct one, as it dispatched a 25,000-man expeditionary force to support the Allies. It was a remarkable step, best understood as one looks at the historical evolution of South America's largest nation.

After wrecking the British cruiser HMS Exeter *so badly that it had to limp into Port Stanley harbor in the Falklands in December 1939, German battleship* Graf Spee *found herself cornered in the Rió de la Plata by British Commodore Harwood's cruisers* Ajax *and* Achilles. *As a result the Graf Spee was herself so seriously damaged that her captain von Langsdorff decided to scuttle her. While the ship was going down, he spread a German flag on the floor of his cabin and shot himself. His crew was subsequently interned in Buenos Aires.*

Characteristic colonial street of the delightful old town of Colonia Sacramento shows adobe-style houses evoking the former Portuguese presence in Uruguay's history.

Solitary cow ruminates outside Colonia's now disused bullring.

A magnificent panoramic view of Colonia.

The lighthouse in Colonia offers a fine view of the old town.

A glinting gold conquistador in armor is a favorite backdrop for visitors' photographs.

In the port of Montevideo, capital of Uruguay, this statue of a sturdy stevedore highlights the country's traditional role as an exporter of beef and primary products.

Statue of Giuseppe Garibaldi in Montevideo, where the Italian patriot spent six years from 1842 to 1848.

*Behind the café parasols and trees of Plaza Constitución,
the twin towers of Montevideo's Cathedral face across to the Cabildo, the city's Town Hall.*

*The ornate fountain in the center of Plaza Constitución commemorates the famous 1823 Grito de Libertad or
"Call for Liberty" of the illustrious 33 Uruguayan patriots.*

Nazca textile created 1,500 years ago reveals the remarkable ability of ancient Andean artists to combine simultaneously figurative and non-figurative motifs in the same composition.

20th-century constructivist painting by Uruguayan artist Joaquín Torres-García, "La Locomotora," reveals his avowed debt to pre-Columbian compositional designs.

(Above) Plaza Independencia offers a garden in the midst of the city;
behind is the classical Palacio Estevez (1907),
which served as Government House until 1985.

(Right) Equestrian statue of national hero José Gervasio Artigas
above the Artigas Mausoleum in Montevideo's Plaza Independencia
represents the epic early 19th-century struggles for
independence of La Banda Oriental or
"Eastern bank of the River," as Uruguay was then called.

Ornate Palacio Salvo (1927) towers over Plaza Independencia.

Neoclassical portico columns grace the facade of Montevideo's Solis Theater, once host to such international performers as tenor Enrico Caruso, actress Sarah Bernhardt and ballet dancers Pavlova and Nijinsky.

The Legislature building, like much of the architecture of southern South America, echoes 19th-century European neoclassical styles.

*Montevideo's sweeping Malecón provides the opportunity for a pleasant stroll along the waterfront,
past the U.S. Embassy to the National Fine Arts Museum in the Parque Rodó.*

Dynamic gaucho statue on Montevideo's Avenida 18 de Julio captures the dash and bravado of South America's romanticized searchers for freedom on the pampas.

The buildings and garden of the Museo Municipal de Bellas Artes Juan Manuel Blanes, in Montevideo's Prado suburb, have an ambiance that is reminiscent of an Italian country villa.

Baroque garden statuary in the Blanes Museum.

Inner patio of the Blanes Museum, embellished in Italianate style.

*Huge painting by Juan Manuel Blanes portrays the dramatic moment in which
33 Uruguayan patriots of Lavalleja swear the famous* Juramento (Oath) *in 1823.*

This oil painting entitled "Dusk" by Juan Manuel Blanes is characteristic of his often poignant representations of gaucho life.

20th-century "Candombé" painting by Uruguay's Pedro Figari is an unusual depiction of a black protagonist in the art of southern South America.

CHAPTER VIII Brazil's Unique Mixture of *Mestizaje,* Monarchs, Macumba and Modernism

Beholding Rió's Wonders

I've never sailed the Amazon,
I've never reached Brazil
But the Don and Magdalena,
They can sail there when they will.

Yes, weekly from Southampton,
Great steamers, white and gold
Go rolling down to Rió
These wonders to behold.
And I'd like to go to Rió
Some day before I'm old.

So wrote Rudyard Kipling, the chronicler of Britain's great imperial age in such books as *If, The Jungle Book* and *Captains Courageous.* Kipling never did get to Rió de Janeiro, but if he had he would have found incomparable wonders, not only spectacular scenery and an incredible population mix, but also an emperor, the only monarch of the Americas, in the person of Dom Pedro II, who ruled until abdicating in 1889 after a coup led by progressive military officers.

When Napoleon invaded Portugal in the early 1800s, the Portuguese court, with a retinue of 15,000 lords, ladies and servants, sailed off to be a government in exile in Rió de Janeiro, capital of Portugal's colony of Brazil. A fantastic event! One can imagine the pomp and pageantry of those Lisbon courtiers, their civilized manners and pastel crinolines suddenly juxtaposed with Brazil's wild and savage beauty, its often mephitic heat and the pulsing energy and liveliness of its exotic black, mulatto, *zambi* and mestizo population.

Magnificent Coastline

As they sailed past the Fortress at the entrance to Guanabara Bay, they would have been as spellbound by its majestic tropical splendor as those who are fortunate enough to sail into Rió today. For more than 25 kilometers, a magnificent coastline strung out between Niteroi in the north and Gavea in the south winds along a seafront of gracious parks and striking esplanades embellished, in Portuguese style, with patterned mosaics.

Colorful sights flash by: Santos Dumont airport, the Museum of Modern Art, Flamengo Park, Botafogo and then the promontory from which the spectacular 1,200-foot high Pão de Açúcar—Sugar Loaf—rises so dramatically. The legendary beaches begin here: Praia Vermelha, Leme, Copacabana, Arpoador, Ipanema, Leblon, Vidigal and Gavea, with the celebrated Freitas Lake and Botanical Gardens set back behind Ipanema and Leblon. This is the world of the *Carioca,* an Indian word which originally meant the "House of the White Man."

Exhilarating Mystique

There never has been a city quite like Rió. Pollution in the water, *favela* shantytowns clinging to the hills, cases of police brutality against vagrant children and an endemic poverty have dimmed some of the traditional luster. The prevalence of poverty makes discretion advisable in one's appearance; flaunting ostentatious jewelry or carrying wallets in visible back pockets offers unfair temptation to many people for whom existence is a daily struggle.

But these are inevitable problems of numerous contemporary urban metropolises, and they do little to diminish the excitement, exhilaration and mystique of a city that glows like many of the gems for which Brazil is so deservedly famed. The mid-20th century was when the glamour and romance of Rió first took on an international aura. There was Fred Astaire in *Flying Down to Rió*; the flamboyance of Carmen Miranda; the cavorting of a new chic jet set; the music of Carlos Jobim and the words by Vinicius de Moraes immortalizing the insouciant "Girl from Ipanema;" a strange and magical film, *Black Orpheus*, which was inspired by Albert Camus; and always the pulsing rhythm and exhilaration of the annual Carnival.

2000: Brazil's Portuguese Origins and 500th Anniversary

Just as 1992 was an occasion for celebration, marking as it did 500 years after the arrival of Columbus in the New World, so was the dawn of 2000 a momentous event for Portuguese and Brazilians alike, for it heralded the 500th anniversary of the discovery of Brazil in 1500.

PEDRO ALVARES CABRAL

When Pope Alexander VI designated a north/south line in the Atlantic in 1494 that assigned lands west of the line to Spain, and those east of it to Portugal (a line that now runs roughly from Brazil's Belém south to Porto Alegre), no one could have foreseen that, a mere six years later, Alvares Cabral would not only discover Brazil, but find that its huge northeastern territory fell well within the Portuguese domain! Eventually all of Brazil became Portuguese, which explains why Brazil is the only country of South America that does not speak Spanish.

Three Capitals: Bahía (1500–1763); Rió (1763–1960) and Brasilia

For more than 300 years, Brazil would be a Portuguese colony, ruled by kings and queens from Lisbon until it became independent in 1821. For the next 68 years, it would be a Brazilian monarchy, finally becoming an independent republic in 1889.

Until 1763 its capital was Salvador da Bahía, but by the 18th century, as the fabulous gold and gems of Minas Gerais Province west of Rió produced untold wealth, it was more logical to move the capital to Rió, where officials could supervise exports to guarantee receipt of the royal quota. By 1960, however, Brazil had its third capital, Brasilia, 1,200

In a proud plaza in Portugal's hillside town of Santarem, the sword and cross are reminders of the feat of Pedro Alvares Cabral, founder in 1500 of a Brazil that in the year 2000 celebrated its 500th anniversary.

kilometers to the northwest of Rió. The brainchild of President Juscelino Kubitschek, Brasilia became a "pole of growth" to open up the interior and to relievę the overcrowding and over-taxing of Rió's facilities. Its location in scrub flatlands, the "space age" buildings disposed along a two-axis configuration, and the innovative genius of architect Oscar Niemeyer and city planner Lucio Costa, created a stunning mood of fantasy reflecting South America's "marvel of the real."

The Colonial Era: "Late Baroque Gold" in the 1600s and 1700s

Rió de Janeiro offers an exciting panoramic synthesis of three different ages of Brazilian life. Colonial secular architecture up to 1821 includes the old fort at the entrance to Guanabara Bay, and the Carioca Aqueduct, known locally as the Arcos de Lapa, a 36-arched stone structure built in 1723 to carry water from hilly Santa Teresa down to lower areas. Religious institutions of such orders as Jesuits and Franciscans proliferated during these early years, and so too did their churches. A few, like São Francisco de Paolo, reveal the late 18th-century light and airy decorative style known as rococo, but most tend to unabashedly lavish baroque interiors.

The São Antonio Convent, begun in 1608, is probably the oldest, while the São Bento Monastery offers a magnificent view of Guanabara Bay. The Nossa Senhora da Gloria do Outeiro, so called because it is on a small hill, dates from the 1720s, and the imposing Candelaria Church, whose spacious dome and striking towers are very visible in the downtown area, from 1787. Perhaps the most opulently decorated is the São Francisco da Penitencia Church, which amply fulfills the Portuguese dictate that the *igrega dourada*, should be almost entirely covered in gold.

So much so, that Umberto Eco in *Foucault's Pendulum* writes of Brazilian colonial churches with "sacristies sick with gold and pewter" and Christs writhing in pain "in a glow of late baroque gold." Some of the carved figures have distorted faces, perhaps a deliberate visual satire by native workmen who resented their wealthy Portuguese masters.

The 19th Century

This was a time that once again evokes the sense of marvelous reality, a period crowded with remarkable events. In 1821 the Portuguese monarchy was superseded by a Brazilian one; two emperors—Pedro I and Pedro II—reigned until a liberally inspired military coup in 1889 ushered in the Brazilian Republic. This period contributed its own imprint to Rió de Janeiro.

Before Dom João VI returned to Lisbon to assume the Portuguese throne in 1821, he made one enduring contribution to Rió—the magnificent Botanical Gardens west of Freitas Lake. Built in 1808, they include an almost 800-meter long avenue of royal palms, huge Victoria Regis water lilies with a six-meter diameter, and exotic products like clove and nutmeg from Portugal's colonies in the East Indies.

Other striking 19th-century accomplishments testify to Brazilian individualism. Notable are the National Library, the Fine Arts Museum, the Rui Barbosa mansion containing the memorabilia of the man who wrote Brazil's first constitution, and the striking marble and granite Catete Palace, the residence of Brazilian presidents from 1889 to 1954 and now the Muséu da República.

Chácara do Ceu and Santa Teresa

Especially delightful is the Chácara do Ceu Museum, from 1894 to 1968 the residence of Raymundo Ottoni de Castro Maya. Remodeled in 1954, the Museum houses a superb collection of Brazilian, French impressionist and modern paintings. Its location in Santa Teresa makes a visit there especially pleasant. Santa Teresa, with its charming wooded hills, cobbled streets, stone steps and often ornate *belle époque* architecture, has a tranquil air that provides an agreeable contrast to Rió's often agitated exuberance.

Simplified Rio De Janeiro South

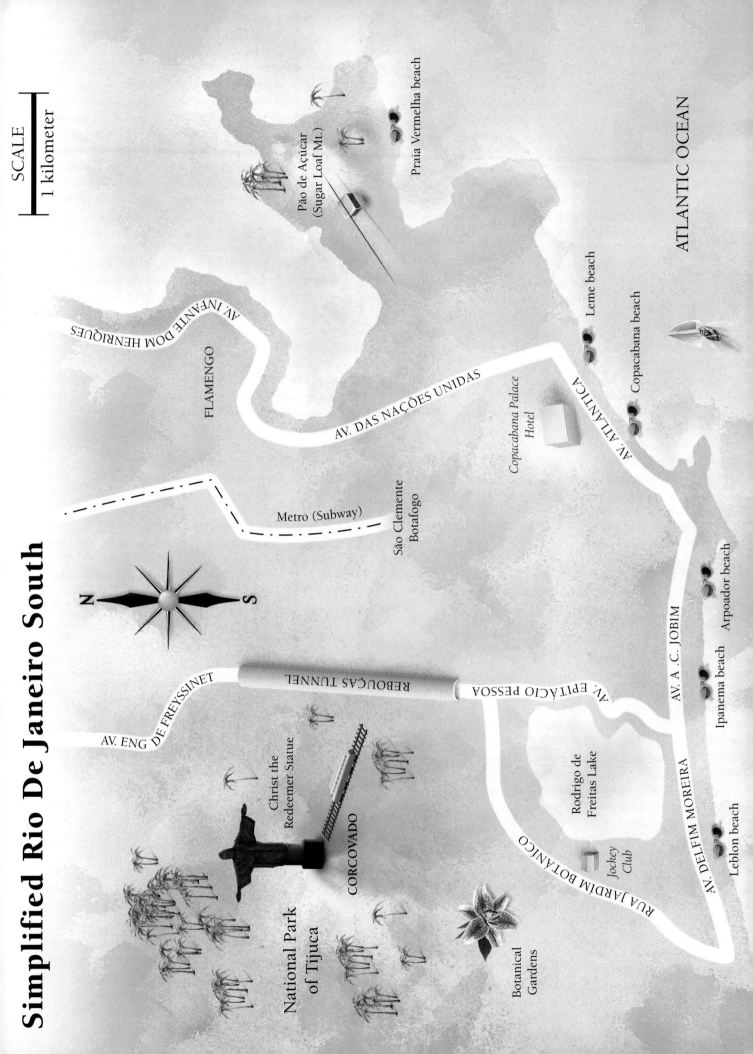

SCALE
1 kilometer

N S

ATLANTIC OCEAN

Praia Vermelha beach

Pão de Açúcar
(Sugar Loaf Mt.)

AV. INFANTE DOM HENRIQUES

FLAMENGO

AV. DAS NAÇÕES UNIDAS

Metro (Subway)

São Clemente
Botafogo

Copacabana Palace
Hotel

AV. ATLANTICA

Leme beach

Copacabana beach

AV. ENG DE FREYSSINET

REBOUÇAS TUNNEL

AV. EPITACIO PESSOA

Christ the
Redeemer Statue

CORCOVADO

National Park
of Tijuca

Rodrigo de
Freitas Lake

Jockey
Club

RUA JARDIM BOTANICO

Botanical
Gardens

AV. DELFIM MOREIRA

AV. A .C. JOBIM

Arpoador beach

Ipanema beach

Leblon beach

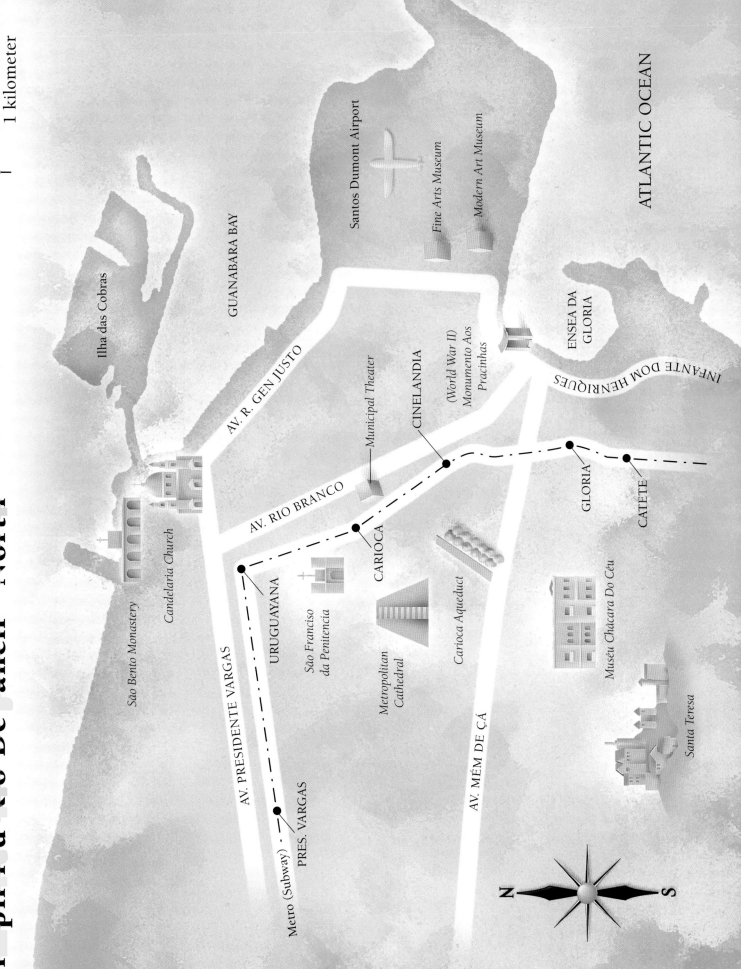

1 kilometer

ATLANTIC OCEAN

Santos Dumont Airport

Fine Arts Museum

Modern Art Museum

GUANABARA BAY

Ilha das Cobras

AV. R. GEN JUSTO

Municipal Theater

CINELANDIA

(World War II)
Monumento Aos
Pracinhas

ENSEA DA
GLORIA

INFANTE DOM HENRIQUES

São Bento Monastery

Candelaria Church

AV. RIO BRANCO

CARIOCA

GLORIA

CATETE

AV. PRESIDENTE VARGAS

URUGUAYANA

São Franciso
da Penitencia

Metropolitan
Cathedral

Carioca Aqueduct

Muséu Chácara Do Céu

AV. MÉM DE CÁ

Santa Teresa

Metro (Subway)
PRES. VARGAS

N

S

Petropolis

The 19th-century monarchical experience embodies much of the marvelous reality of Brazil, and a good way to experience it is to drive up to the summer palace at Petropolis. The drive is a refreshing one, into the cool Serra dos Orgãos mountains north of Rió and past the handsome Quitandinho Hotel.

Dom Pedro II's Palace, now the Muséu Imperial, is in a garden setting replete with statuary and a surprising early bathtub. Inside, the displays of memorabilia include the opulent royal crown embellished with 639 diamonds and 77 pearls.

20th-Century Rió

At the beginning of the 20th century Rió had the look and atmosphere of a European city with its own touch of *belle époque*. Few of the spectacular early 1900 buildings of Avenida Rió Branco remain but the Municipal Theater, a petite version of the Paris opera house, is still there, as is its intriguing first floor Café do Teatro. By 1923, the year that the Hotel Copacabana Palace was completed, chic worldly visitors were ushering in a new era for Rió as the fashionable mecca of the privileged few. In 1931 Rió's most famous landmark, the 100-foot high, 700-ton statue of Christ the Redeemer 2,300 feet atop Corcovado Hill ("the hunchback") was installed by sculptor Paul Landowski. 1938 saw the inauguration of the Santos Dumont waterfront airport, and by the mid-1940s Lucio Costa and Le Corbusier had combined their talents to create the famed avant-garde Ministry of Education, with movable louvers to block out the sun and a base consisting of immense concrete pillars.

Although his real name is Antonio Francisco Lisboa, the sculptor of this figure has always been known as Aleijadinho, the Little Cripple. But there is nothing small about his majestic Brazilian baroque sculptures depicting scenes of the Passion of Christ. Here the "Captive Christ Mocked by Soldiers" displays the compelling pathos and spellbinding sense of realism associated with this late 18th-century artist's work.

Brazilian Imprint

After World War II came an ensemble of eclectic structures that affirmed a local Brazilian imprint, rather than one based on external influences. These included the Metropolitan Cathedral in 1960, a New World creation whose fantastic pyramidal configuration of glowing bronze-gold resembles a classic Mayan temple; the vast Maracanha football stadium (1950), large enough to house 200,000 spectators and a fitting stage for Pele's virtuoso performances; and the Monumento aõs Pracinhas, a pair of soaring columns flanking a tomb that honors the fallen during Brazil's valiant contribution in defeating the Axis in World War II.

The dramatic pose of Christ with outstretched arms, created by the Danish sculptor Bertel Thorvaldsen, who died in 1844, clearly influenced the 1931 sculpture of Christ by Paul Landowski atop Rió de Janeiro's Corcovado Peak.

Calling Getulio Vargas, Brazilian President (1934–1945 and 1950–54) "one of the two men who invented the New Deal," U.S. President Franklin Roosevelt had forged a "special relationship" with Vargas in 1943. It permitted the U.S. to use air bases in the Brazilian northeast, thereby reducing the flight distance to Europe by between 40 and 50 per cent. It also resulted in the dispatch of a Brazilian Expeditionary Force under General Mascarenhas de Moraes, whose 25,000 members fought valiantly in the Italian Campaign.

Arts and Music

In landscape architecture, there were characteristic Brazilian innovations, like world-renowned Roberto Burle Marx's accomplishments in the Museum of Modern Art's gardens, and in the delightful Flamengo Aterro (Landfill) public park. In the plastic arts, Portinari, di Cavalcanti, Amaral, Carybé and Segall revealed a clearly distinctive Brazilian style and temperament in their work. In music, Hector Villa-Lobos probed new dimensions in forms of classical expression. A characteristic work, the "Bachianas Brasileiras," endows the music of Bach with a distinctly Brazilian stamp.

Jorge Amado

And in literature, Salvador da Bahía's Jorge Amado, literary symbol of the pageant of Brazil, captured vividly the sparkle of local life in such celebrated works as *Doña Flor and Her Two Husbands*, and *Gabriela, Clove and Cinnamon*. Their mestizo characters exhibit a *joie de vivre* that is very different in mood from that of the oppressed blacks in an earlier classic work, Gilberto Freyre's *Casa Grande e Senzala* (*The Masters and the Slaves*).

"We are a nation of *mestizaje* (mixed blood), thank God," Amado once said, and he was convinced that it was the blacks who first mixed up this crucible. You just have to hear the sounds of a Brazilian musician, from Villa-Lobos to Dorival Caymi, or look at a painting of Carybé or Di Cavalcanti, or a sculpture of Agudo, or read a poem of Castro Alves or a novel of João Ubaldo Ribeiro, to feel the weight of Africa's contribution.

The Magic of Northeastern Brazil

Jorge Amado is the embodiment of Salvador da Bahía, the northeastern Brazilian city which has inspired much of his writing, and whose picturesque streets, like the Largo do Pelourinho, figure so prominently in his writing. Indeed up here in the north, in colorful cities like Recife, São Luis de Maranhão, Fortaleza and Olinda, the mestizo and black presence is

General João Batista de Mascarenhas commanded the 25,000-man Brazilian Expeditionary force which fought with the Allies in World War II, and in which a future Brazilian President, Castelo Branco, served as a young lieutenant.

"Thank God for our mestizaje," exclaimed celebrated Brazilian writer Jorge Amado, hailing his country's exotic mixed blood heritage of whites, blacks, mulattos and zambis *(those of Indian and black African ancestry). A resident of Salvador da Bahía, Amado is best known for locally inspired works like* Doña Flor and her Two Husbands *and* Gabriela, Clove and Cinnamon.

especially pronounced.

It is the blacks, says Amado, who have "saved us from melancholy and sadness." Black influence is manifest in rhythmic music and dance, especially the samba, which may have originated in Angola's samba, maxixe or frevo. It is apparent in festivals, of which the climax is the annual Carnival, known as *Carnaval.* Beginning on the Friday before, and ending on Ash Wednesday, *Carnaval* is a cathartic release of tensions enhanced by the sensual beat of the music, the torrid gyrations of sinuous bodies and an often total abandonment of inhibitions. Above all, *Carnaval* is the great equalizer, a six-day interlude when the poorest *cariocas* can fantasize as they mix with the élite during the parade of the Samba Schools.

Macumba: Umabamba, Qimbamba, Candomblé

Trance-like states induced during the annual Jemanjá Festival, the martial art known as Capoeira, the cuisine favoring hot peppers, *dende* oil and okra—all these echo the heritage of Africa. Most of all, however, it is the spiritist Macumba cults, and their often bizarre syncretic blend with Catholicism, that makes Brazil so unique.

These cults believe in beneficial contacts with the spirits of gods from another world, reached through mediums who go into ecstatic trances when possessed or visited by spirits. Umabamba has Brazilian gods like the Old Black Slave, a Portuguese language, white benign magic and Qimbamba black destructive magic, all articulated by a medium called an Exu and his prostitute consort Pomba Giral. In Candomblé, especially popular in Salvador da Bahía, the language is African; and deities like Olorun, God of Hunting, are African Yoruba with Christian overlays.

Were it not for the blending and syncretism that have characterized Brazilian life since colonial times, Amado asserted, it "would not have been possible to endure the centuries of misery which still continue: the exploitation, the constant hunger, the *latifundia* (large agricultural and cattle ranching estates and labor on the land), the epidemics, the disproportionate infant mortality, the illiteracy, the political oppression of military dictatorships. . ."

The military dictatorships have gone now, to be followed since 1985 by a succession of civilian presidents. The Brazilian military tradition has been a dichotomous one, with liberal progressivism juxtaposed with entrenched conservatism. Thus when Marshal Hermes Fonseca opposed the monopoly of political power maintained by Minas Gerais and São Paulo states, young lieutenants supporting his ideals battled federal troops on Copacabana Beach in the July 1922 Revolt of the Eighteen of the Fort. Then came the 1924 uprising of Colonel Isidoro Lopes in São Paulo and the famous "Long March" by communist officer Carlos Prestes, which ended in Bolivia in 1927.

By 1964, with President João Goulart exhibiting marked leftist tendencies, the military asserted its tutelary role as guardian of the nation's institutions to stage a coup that removed him from office. The military's subsequent *Linha Dura* (Hard Line) authoritarianism, justified by their need for a strong stand against left-wing terrorism, was generally condoned by Washington; there was little sympathy for terrorists who kidnapped U.S. Ambassador to Brazil, Burke Elbrick, and Washington was apprehensive about the threat of communist expansion throughout South America.

The positive accomplishments of military rule were an economic miracle in national growth and development, and the opening up of the Amazon with road networks into the interior. However, this westward expansion was destined to have often disastrous consequences for the habitat of some of the approximately 150 Stone Age peoples inhabiting the Amazon rain forest—peoples like the Yanomanis and Kaiapos, whose often exotic cultural traditions, including the wearing of multicolored feather headdresses, can be appreciated in Rió's Muséu del Indio in Botafogo. Often brutal mistreatment of the Indians by landowners and entrepreneurs of all types continues to be a problem in Brazil's interior, in spite of the efforts of organizations established to protect these ancient peoples and their traditions.

Ecological Damage to the Amazonian Tropical Rain Forest

Opening up the tropical Amazonian rain forest has had one further consequence of potentially disastrous dimensions—the ecological damage to the environment. Slash-and-burn policies to increase available land for agriculture, the contamination of rivers resulting from mineral exploitation and local disdain for environmental concerns continue to endanger numerous species of irreplaceable flora and fauna.

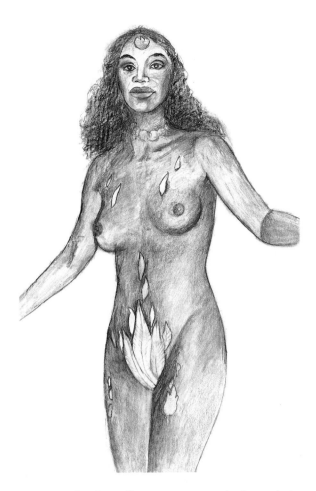

Sultry, sensual and sexually provocative, a samba dancer during Brazil's Lenten carnival displays the charms and exoticism engendered by the country's mixed blood heritage.

Tudo Bem . . . Muito Jeito

But these are concerns far from the mind of the visitor to Rió de Janeiro. The city's burning sun, the tropical scenery, the colorful *feijoada* black bean dishes, the delicious cool *caipirinha* cocktails and the exotic racial blends combine to create a world apart. Romance, a sense of youthfulness, the feline grace of female figures clad only in scanty *tangas*, the tradition of Dr Pitangui's vaunted facial cosmetic surgery, the sheer *joie de vivre* of the people, the unforgettable views from Corcovado or Pão do Açúcar—all these exert their own entrancing spell. In Rió, after all, the key phrase is "*tudo bem!*" ("everything's fine!"); and it always will be, as long as you have the other key Brazilian ingredient, "*muito jeito!*" (skill in solving problems by often unorthodox means).

Conclusion

Rudyard Kipling, though he saw much of the world, never beheld Rió's wonders. Those who are lucky enough to "roll down to Rió" on a great steamer are among the privileged few. For Rió is a city that scintillates, as do the lovely amethysts, aquamarines and tourmalines which endow Brazil with a cachet that is as glittering as it is authentic. "With what pleasure, with what joy, you come into harbors seen for the first time." Constantin Cavafy tells us. And indeed, to sail into Rió de Janeiro is to participate in the marvelous reality of the Americas—to end, perhaps, one voyage, but to envisage many more in this extraordinary and magical continent.

The Corcovado Christ, Rió de Janeiro's most renowned landmark.

View from Corcovado Peak in Rió, with Sugar Loaf Mountain in the background.

Rió beaches — brightly colored parasols, vivid hues and Sugar Loaf Mountain seen in the hazy distance comprise a scene which evokes the mood of Jobim's famous song "Girl from Ipanema."

Picturesque old houses in the Santa Teresa barrio of Rió.

The Copacabana Palace Hotel (1923), recently restored to its former splendor.

Rió Cathedral, in the form of a pyramid.

Fort at entrance to Rió harbor where Italian patriot Garibaldi was once imprisoned.

(Above) The famed Quitandinho Hotel, en route to Petropolis, Dom Pedro II's retreat.

(Left) Romantic statuary in the exotic garden of Petropolis Royal Palace.

The colorful old Largo do Pelourinho section of Salvador da Bahía, seen from the Fundacao Jorge Amado Building.

*The steep incline of Rua Luiz Vianna Filho,
in the old city of Salvador da Bahía in northeastern Brazil.*

Large cross in front of Bahía's Igrega de São Francisco church.

Olinda: brilliant colors distinguish the artisan market.

Olinda: Igrega do Carmo on a hill.

Palacio da Justicia, São Luis, recognizable by its stately elegance and the soft pastel rose facade, which combines charmingly with the flamboyant decoration of its windows.

(Above) Handsome architecture in the Praça de Independencia, Recife.

(Right) The imposing Cathedral, São Luis (Maranhão).